I0760186

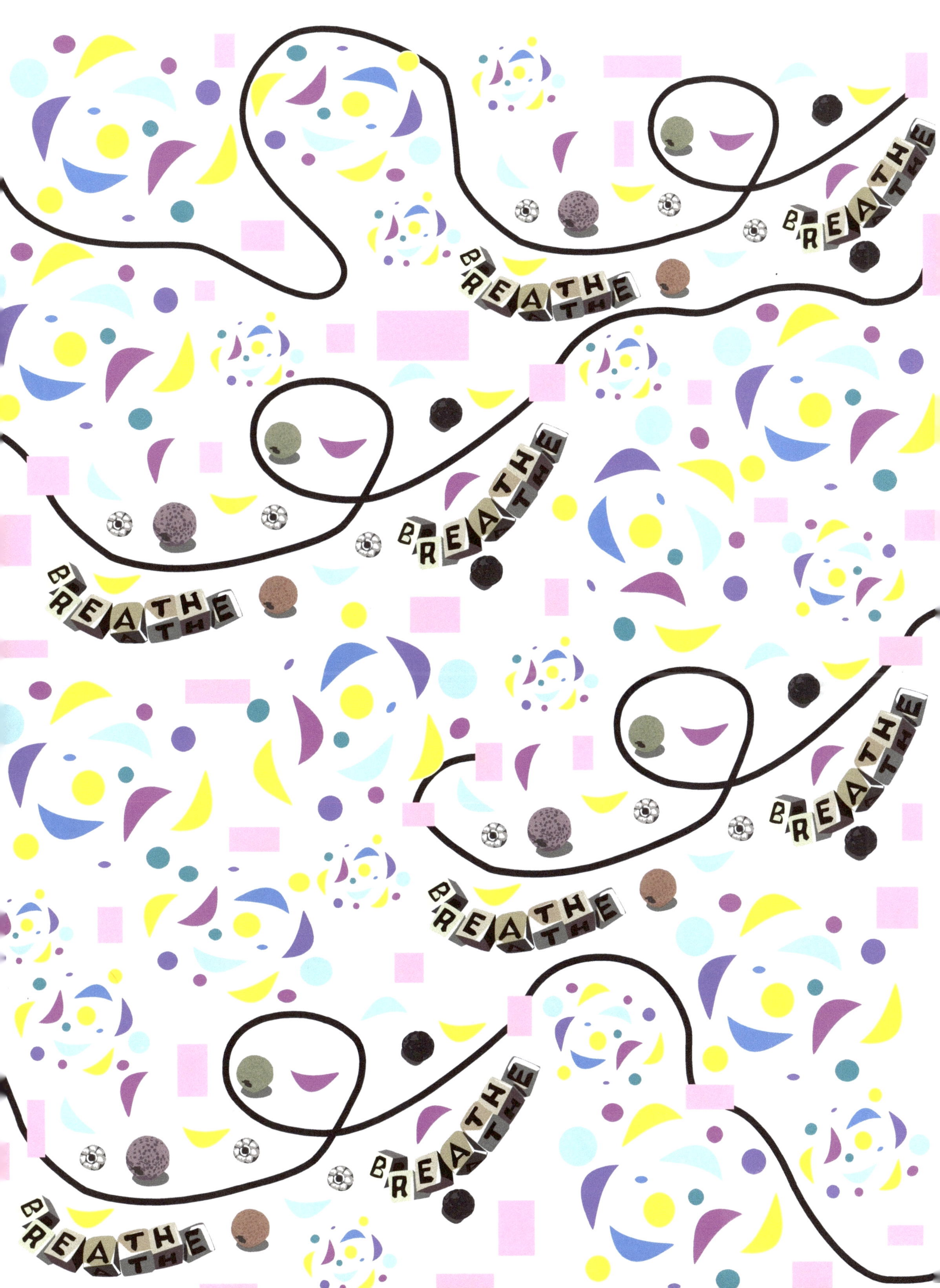
BREATHE
BREATHE
BREATHE
BREATHE
BREATHE
BREATHE
BREATHE
BREATHE

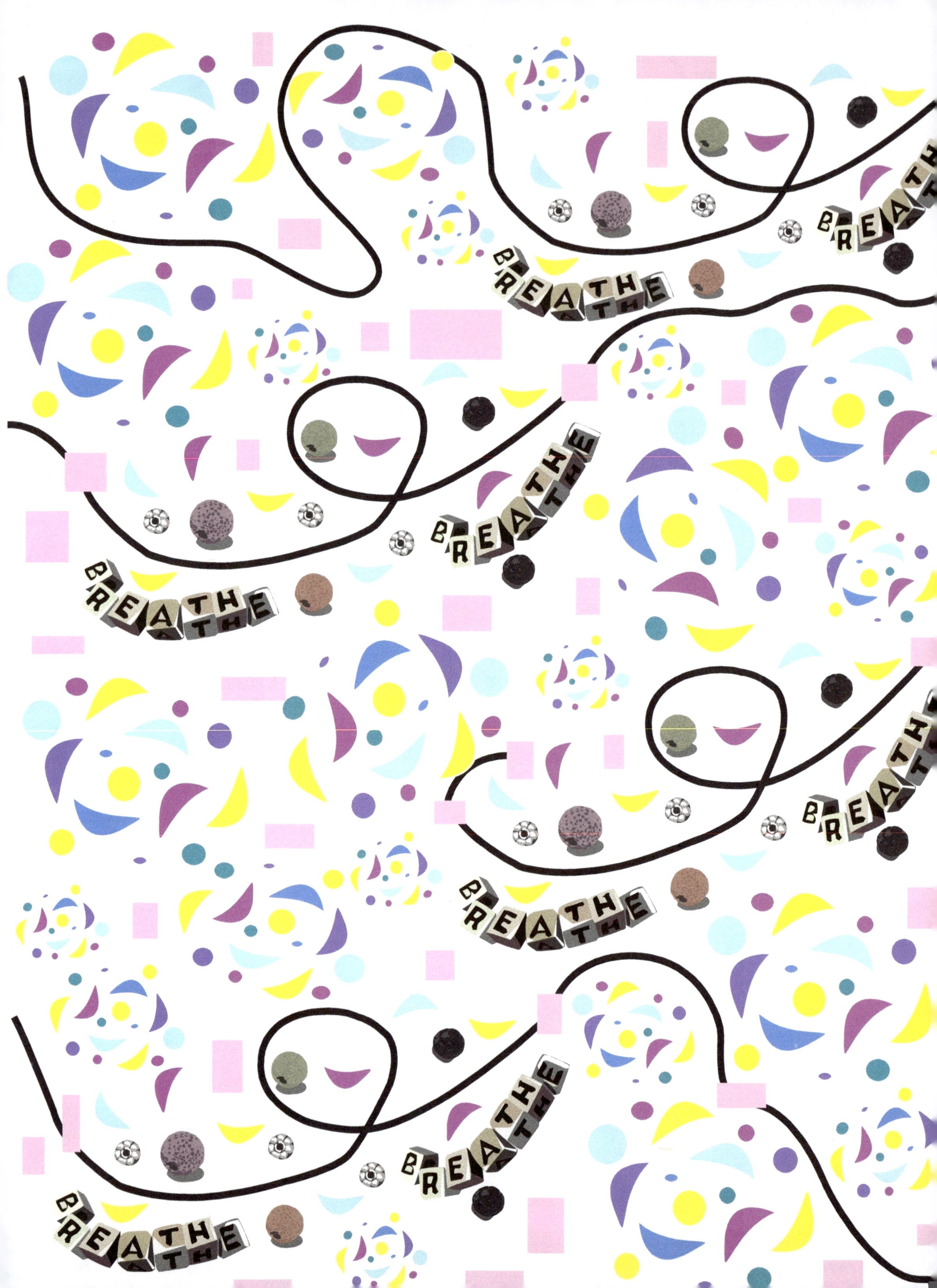
BREATHE
BREATHE
BREATHE
BREATHE
BREATHE
BREATHE

Publisher: TRY Speaking Up Media & Publishing, LLC.

ISBN: 979-8-9885226-3-8
Please be advised that this self-care guide is for educational purposes only, and is not all inclusive to all of the forms of self-care that can be helpful to each person. Please note this book should be used as a guide, and not all inclusive to all things mental health, self-care and health. This guide is not to be used in place of professional services (i.e., therapy, seeing a health professional, etc.). This guide should be used along with other methods of self-care for educational purposes and entertainment solely.


Made in the USA

**WWW.TRYTUTORINGSERVICES.COM**

@TRY.TUTORING.COPING.SOLUTIONS

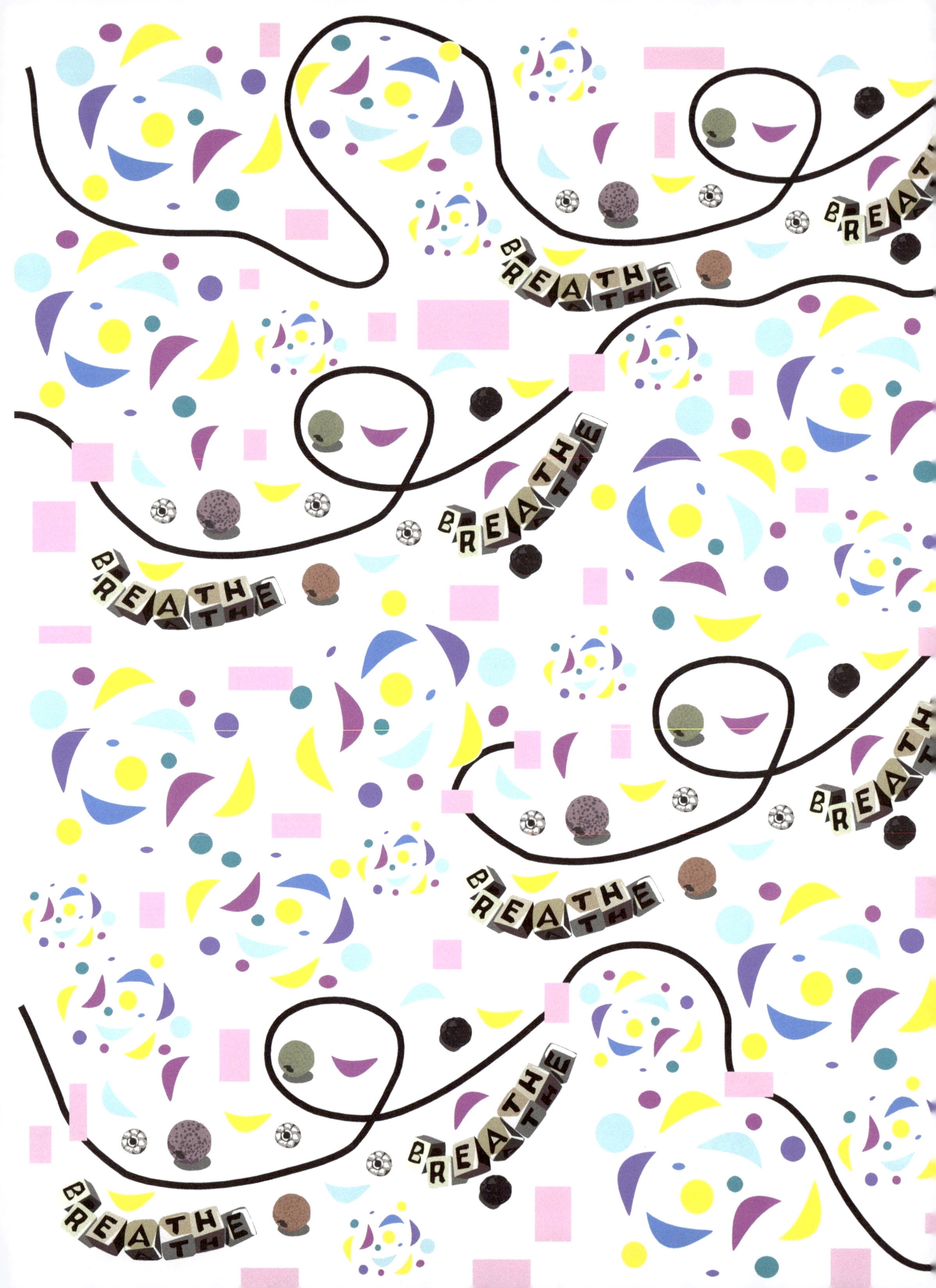
BREATHE
BREATHE
BREATHE
BREATHE
BREATHE
BREATHE

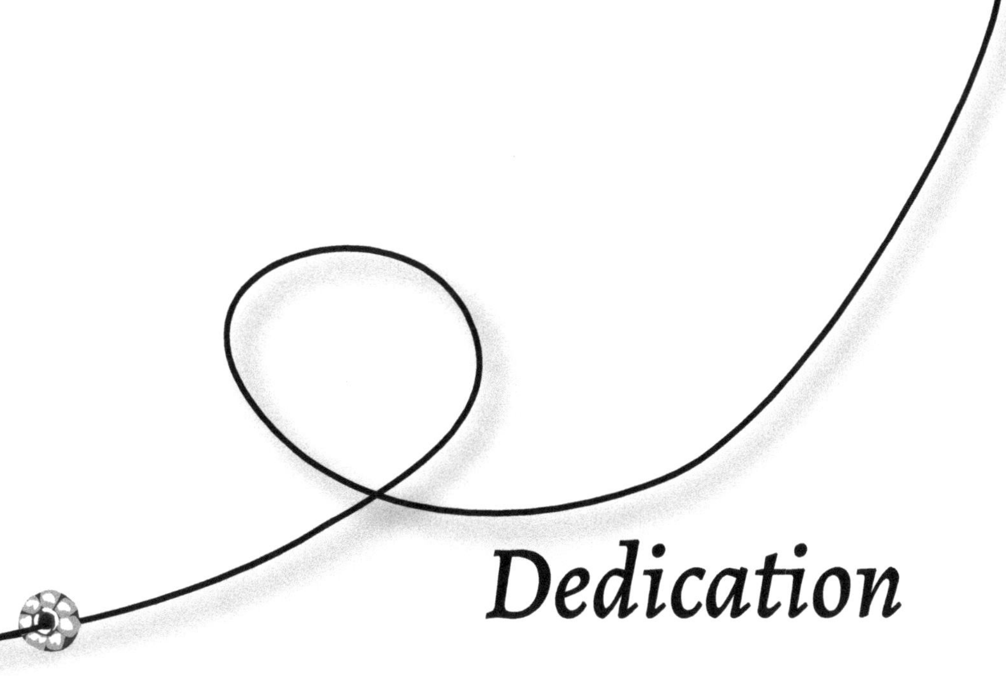

# *Dedication*

*This guide is dedicated to anyone who has struggled with anxiety… who have difficulty expressing and explaining your challenge with anxiety to others with words.*

*You are not invisible.*

*I see you.*

*Signed,*

*Latasha Strawder*

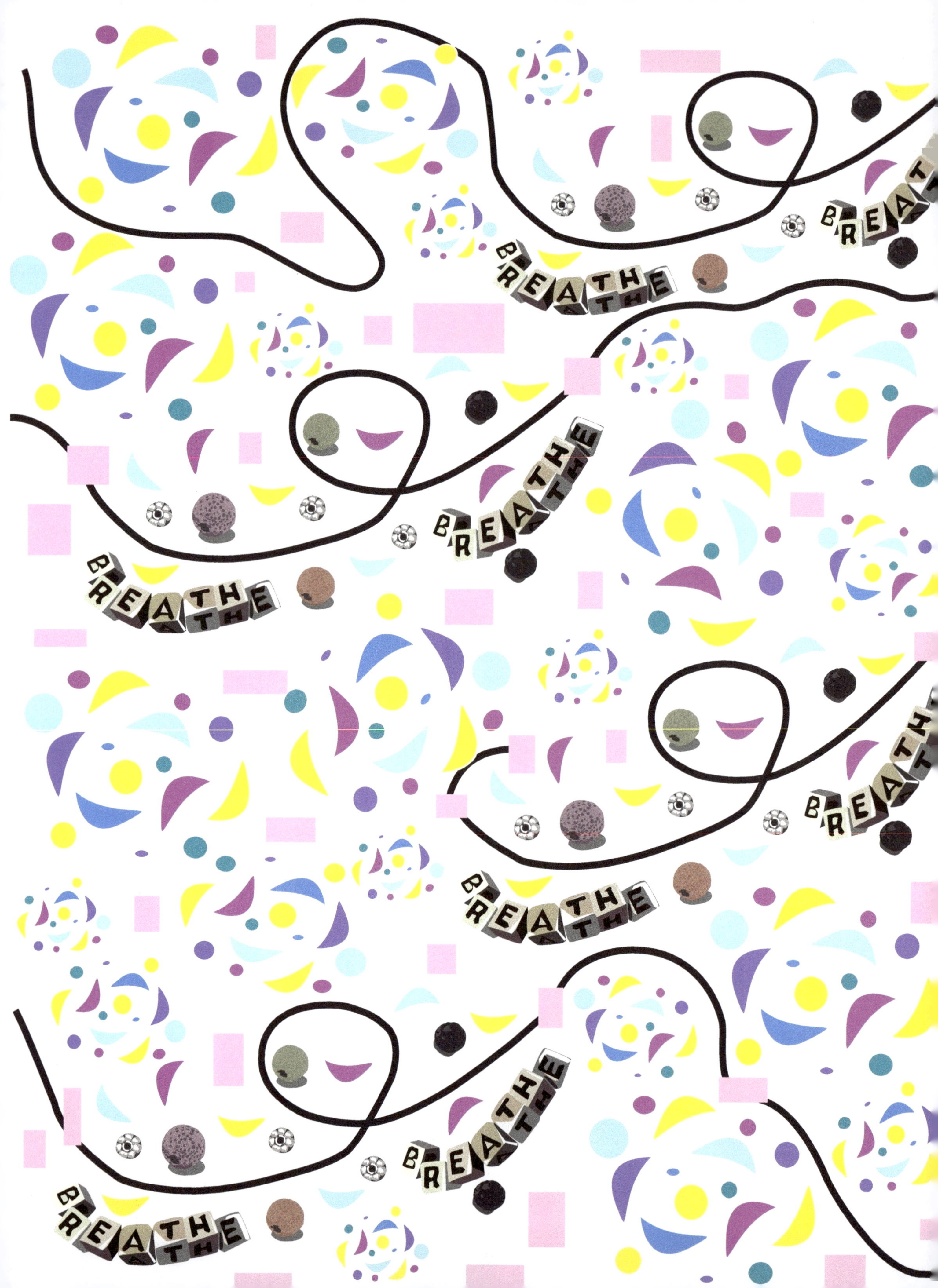
BREATHE
BREATHE
BREATHE
BREATHE
BREATHE
BREATHE

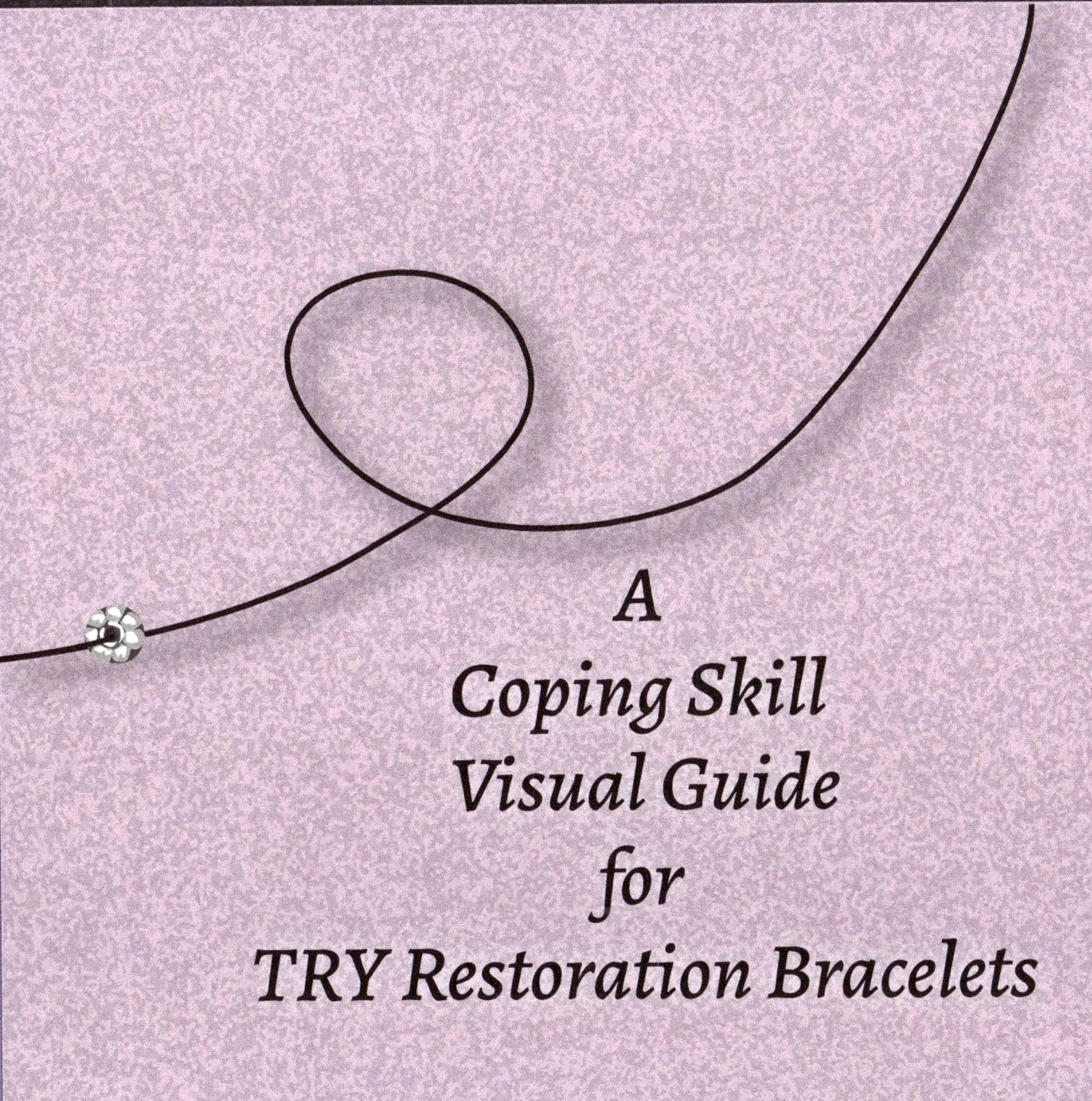

# *A Coping Skill Visual Guide for TRY Restoration Bracelets*

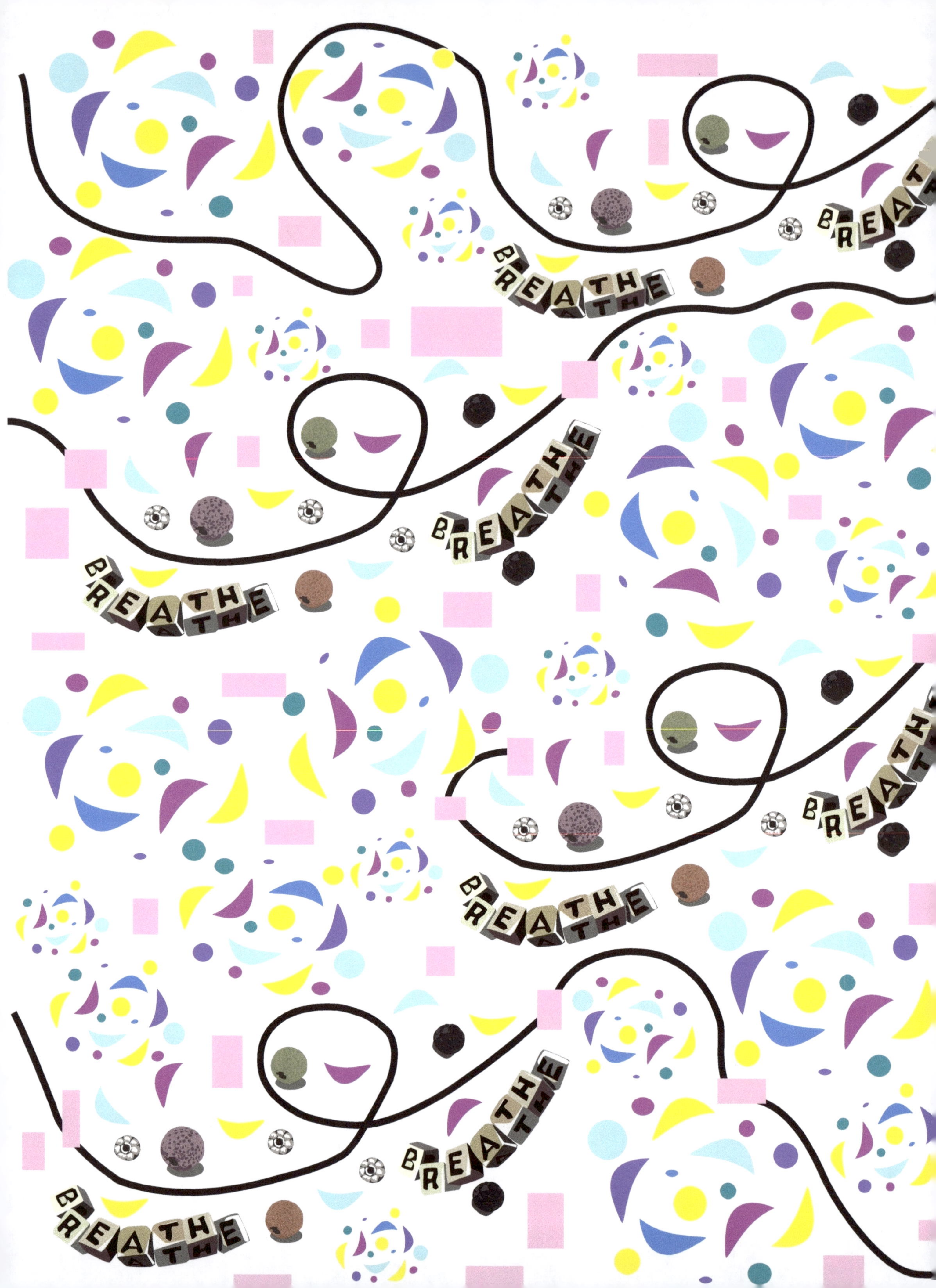
BREATHE
BREATHE
BREATHE
BREATHE
BREATHE
BREATHE
BREATHE
BREATHE

Anxiety in the most extreme form can make one feel as if they are suffocating, can't breath, or even like they may be dying. This often occurs during an anxiety and/or panic attack. It is important to talk with a medical professional to seek help to manage these symptoms. Some may choose to utilize a series of resources to manage anxiety which may include, but are not limited to psychotropic medication, mental health therapy, exercise, herbs, aromatherapy, meditation and more. These resources are often utilized together and some choose to utilize them separately. As no one is the same, nor is there a one-size-fits-all method, it is important to find the best resolutions and develop your own unique plan to help improve your anxiety. Life can feel like it is moving very quickly on a minute-by-minute basis. It is important to take some time to evaluate or reevaluate the best method to help with improving your life for the better. Take some time to process what it is that you need. Take time to restore yourself by getting the support you believe would be the most helpful for your unique mental health journey. It can be scary to stop and slow down, as the routine you've been on has become a normal part of your journey. But maybe it's about time to restore yourself to a more healthier lifestyle. It's Okay to TRY something new to improve your mental health for the better. It just may be one of the best decisions of your life.

Take time to

restore

**Yourself...TRY!**

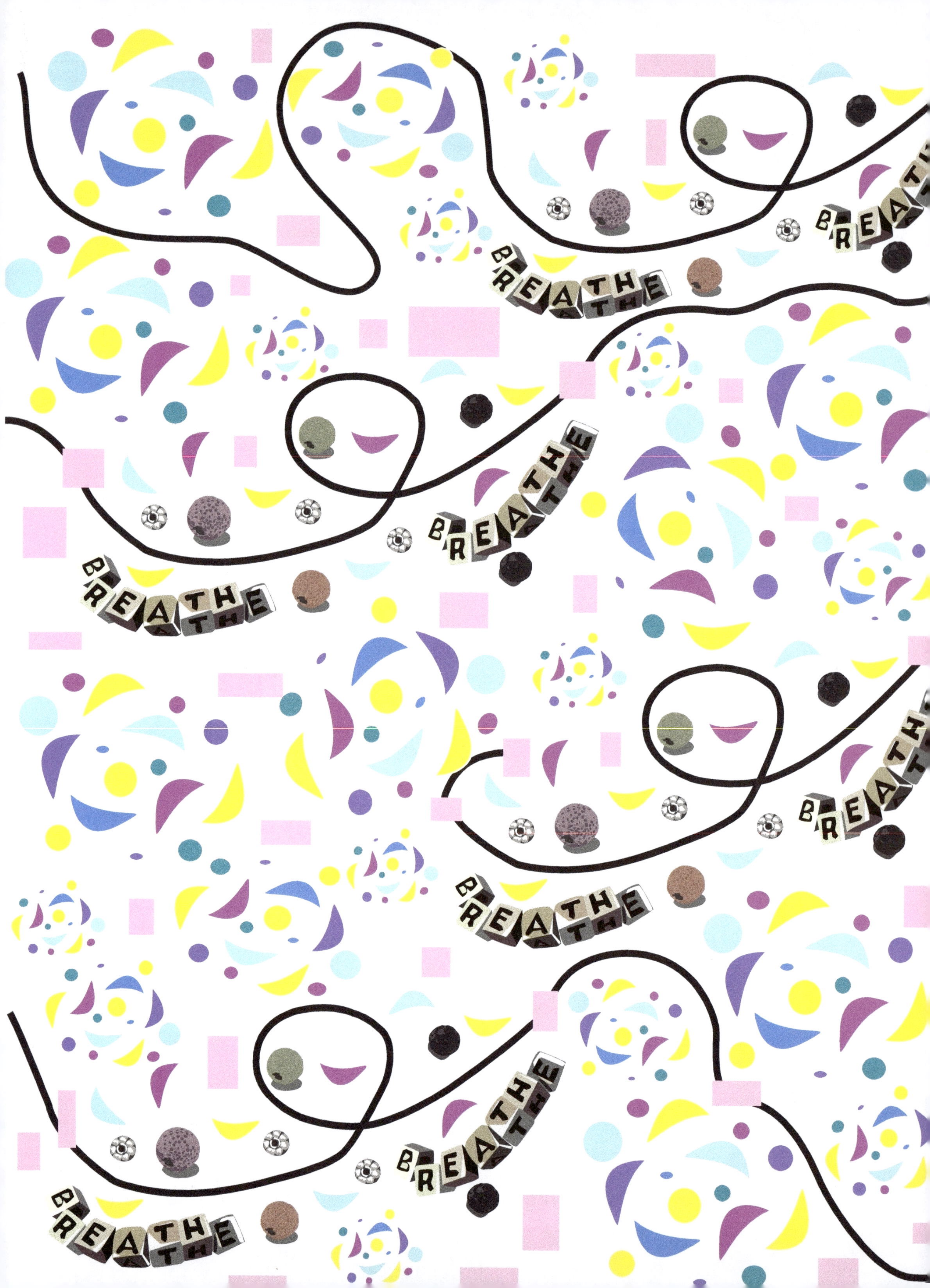
BREATHE
BREATHE
BREATHE
BREATHE
BREATHE
BREATHE

One of the ways to help restore oneself is to use healthy coping skills. An unhealthy coping skill is when you utilize a way of coping that can make your mental health worst (e.g., avoiding conversations that need to be had, internalizing things, self-medicating, drugs, alcohol, etc.) and engaging in other risky behaviors as a way of not dealing with life stressors or confront things head on. Instead, a person may choose to engage in unhealthy coping to help them forget what's causing their mental health to decline in the first place. A healthy coping skill is when you utilize a way of coping that is healthy. One would first acknowledge the feeling, emotion, thought, or behavior that are present in their life that are causing distress. Instead of ignoring or not thinking about it (unhealthy), you acknowledge it is there or that it is taking place in your life. Next, trying to manage them by finding a solution that would make things better for you. It can be hard to follow through on the solutions and you may start to notice the unhealthy coping skills that seemed to "work" for you before, reappear as if they are the best solution (avoidance). Instead of avoiding, TRY to use a healthy coping skill to manage the emotion, thought, feeling and/or behavior that present themselves. It's like learning to develop your emotional muscles by learning to manage your mental state in a new, healthier way. One healthy coping skill you can start with to help stabilize your mood, when you decided not to avoid, is to ground yourself. Grounding is a technique used to help you feel stable before trying to move forward to tackle challenging things in a new, different way, as you may be feeling overwhelmed and are unable to move forward in that moment. Examples of grounding include breathing, identifying all of your senses in the moment (e.g., what do you smell, see, hear, feel, taste), etc.

This is where TRY Restoration Bracelets come in.

You can ground yourself by wearing a bracelet and touching the beads, counting each bead and object on the bracelet, taking deep breaths in between each touch, and you have the option to use aromatherapy by utilizing essential oils on the lava beads (bead with craters that hold the scent of the selected aroma). Continue breathing and using the bracelet until you feel grounded and calm enough to attempt to tackle the hard things. You can wear it so when hard things come up, the bracelet is with you.

This is how you use healthy coping skills!

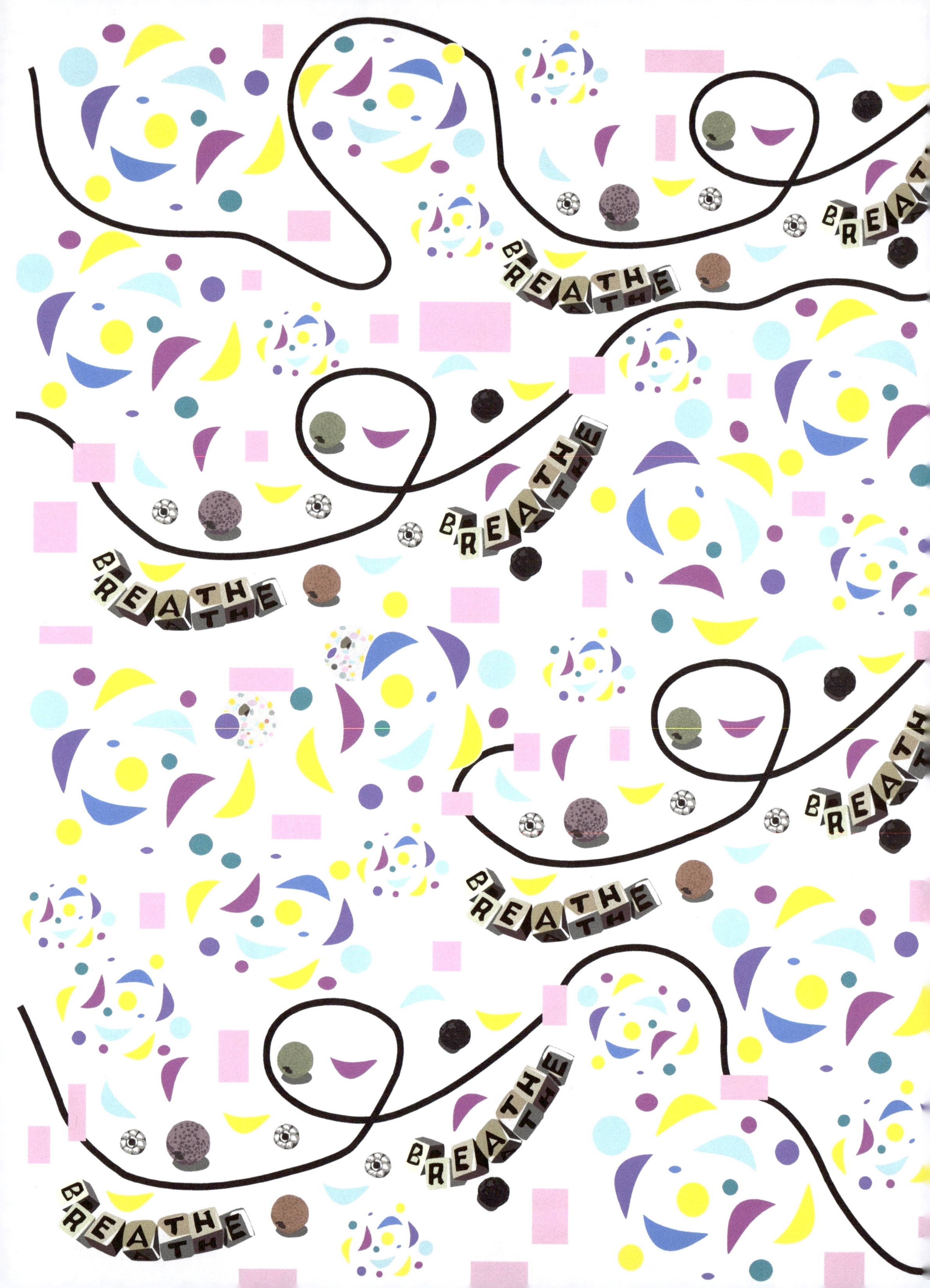
BREATHE
BREATHE
BREATHE
BREATHE
BREATHE
BREATHE

# *Visual Guide*

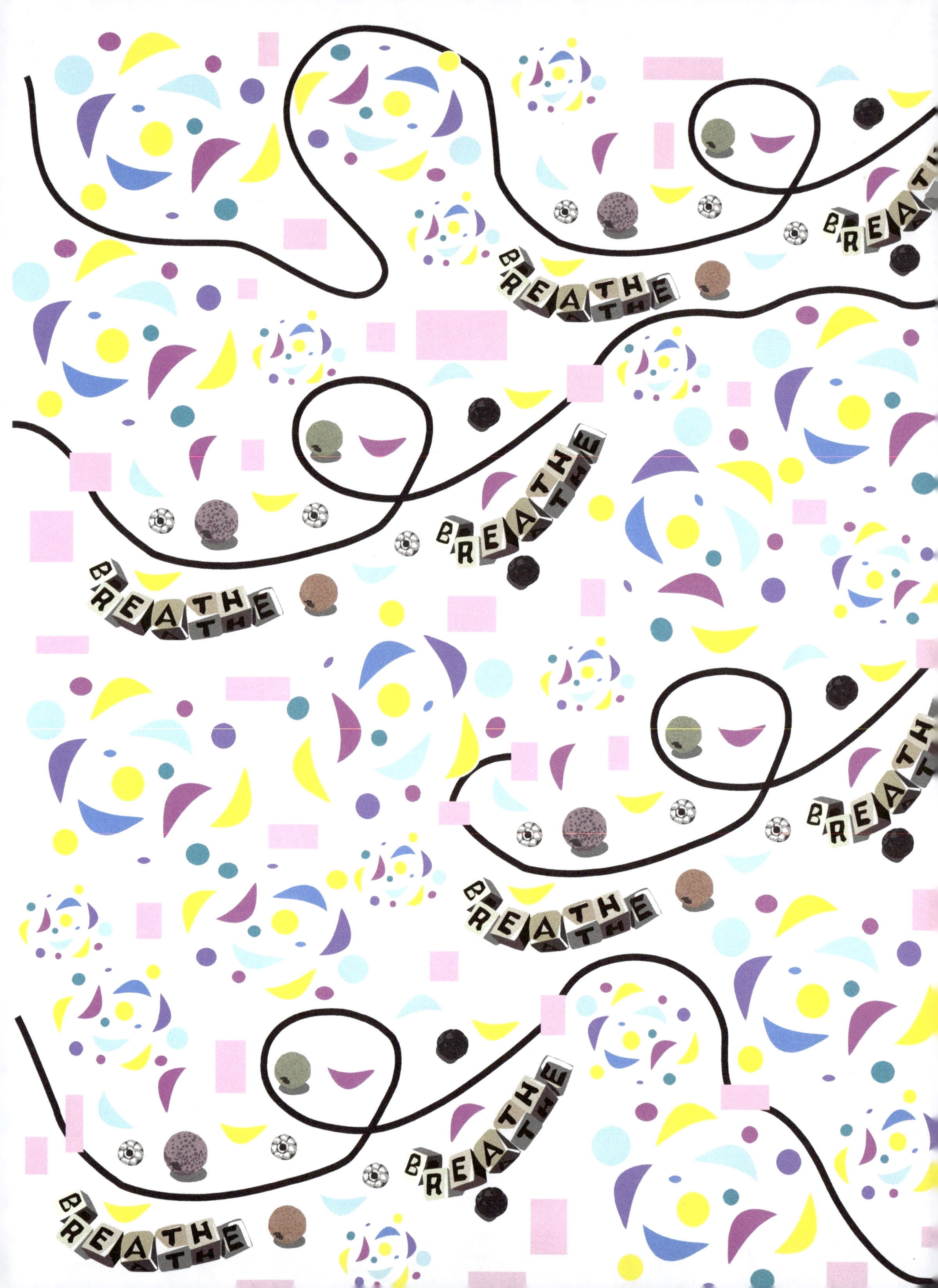
BREATHE
BREATHE
BREATHE
BREATHE
BREATHE
BREATHE

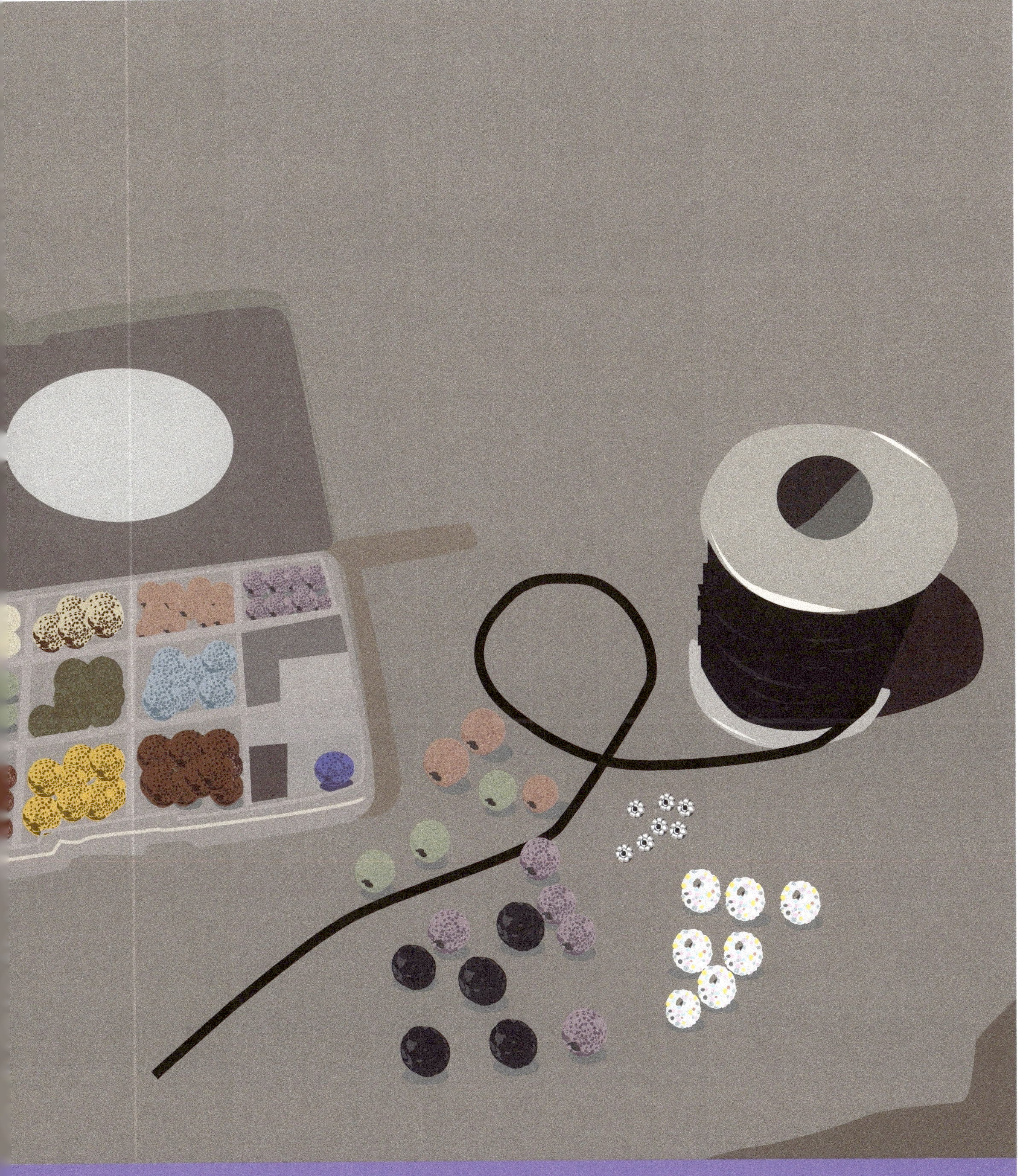

# Step One

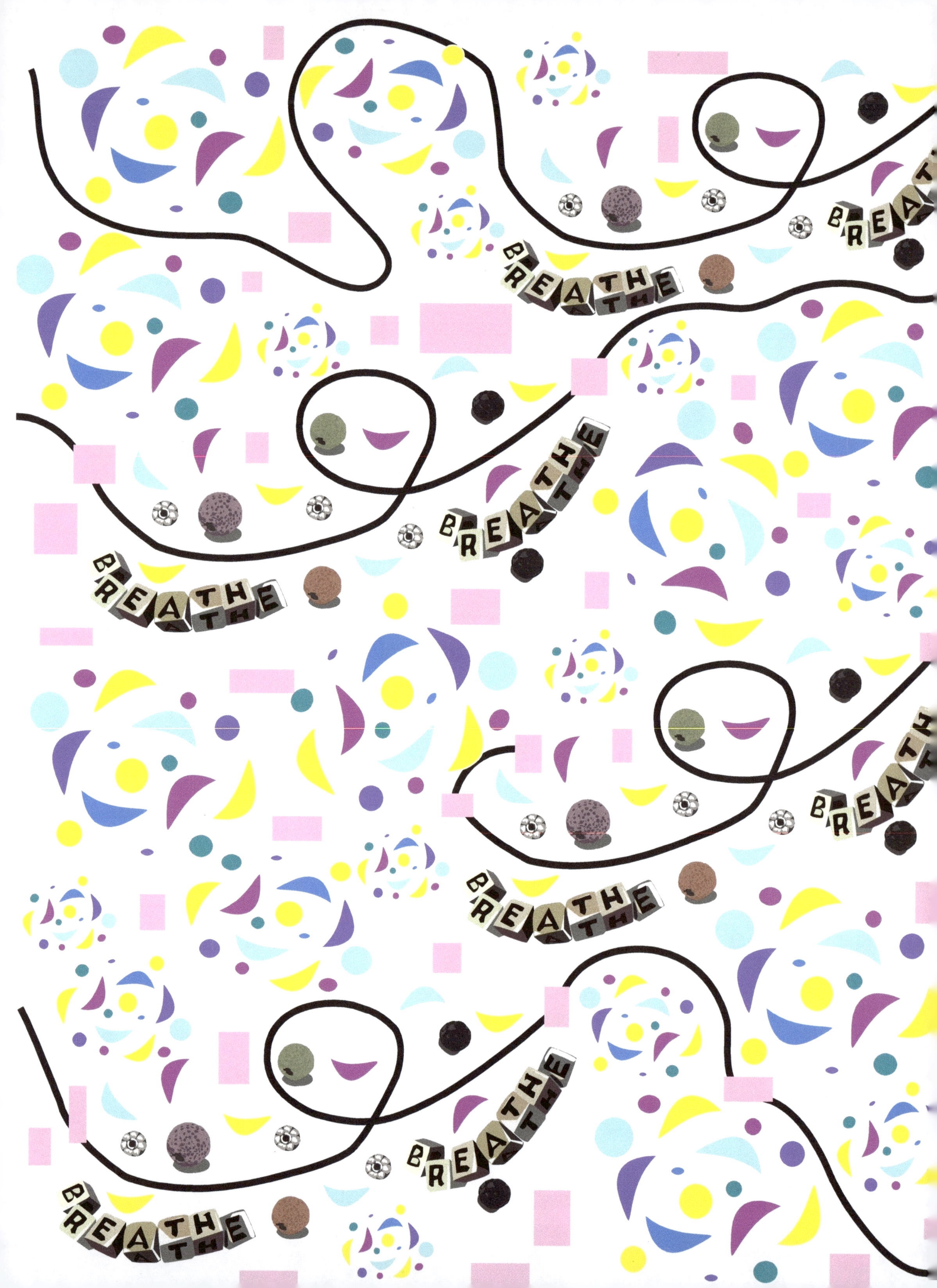
BREATHE
BREATHE
BREATHE
BREATHE
BREATHE
BREATHE

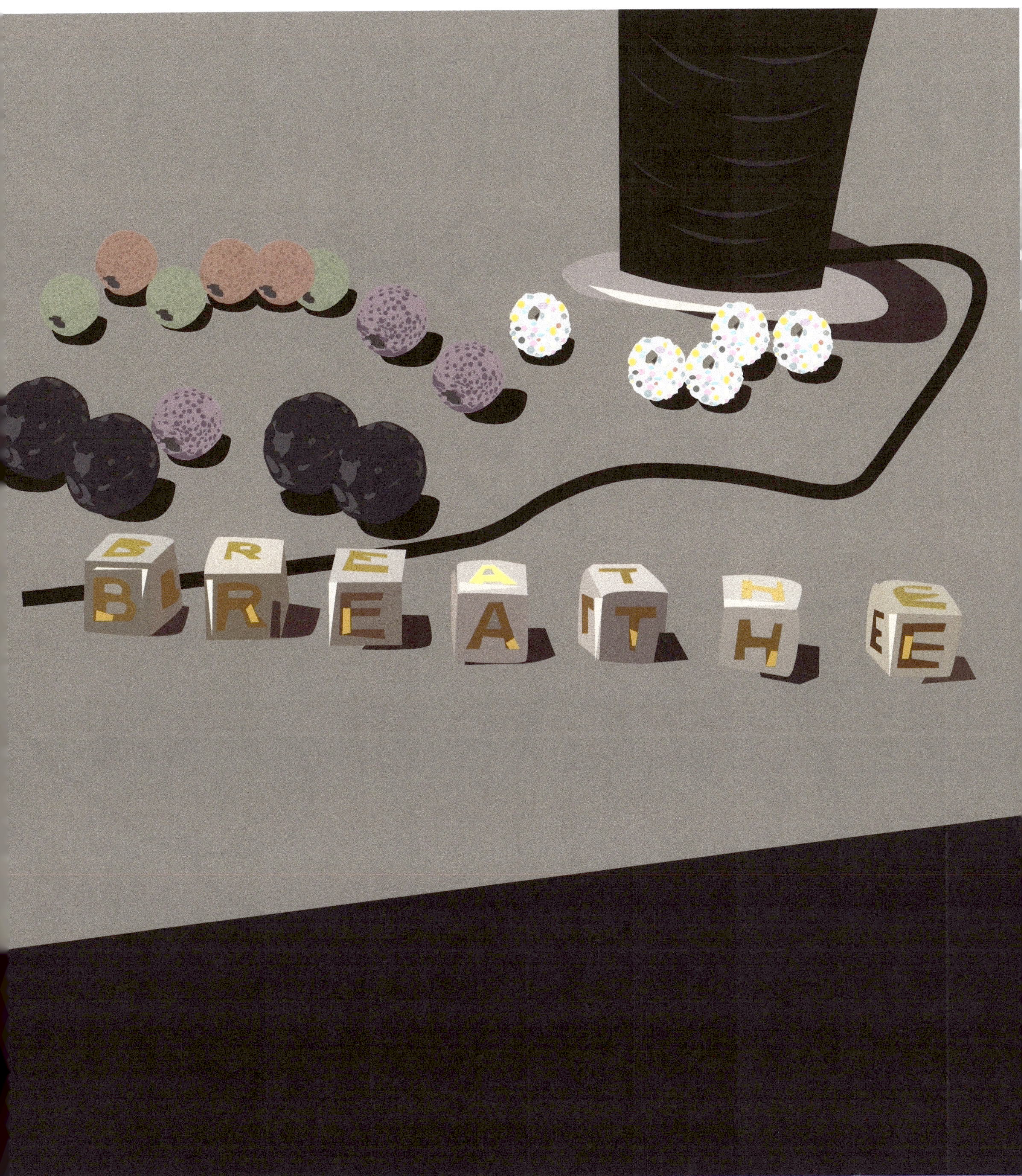


# Step Two

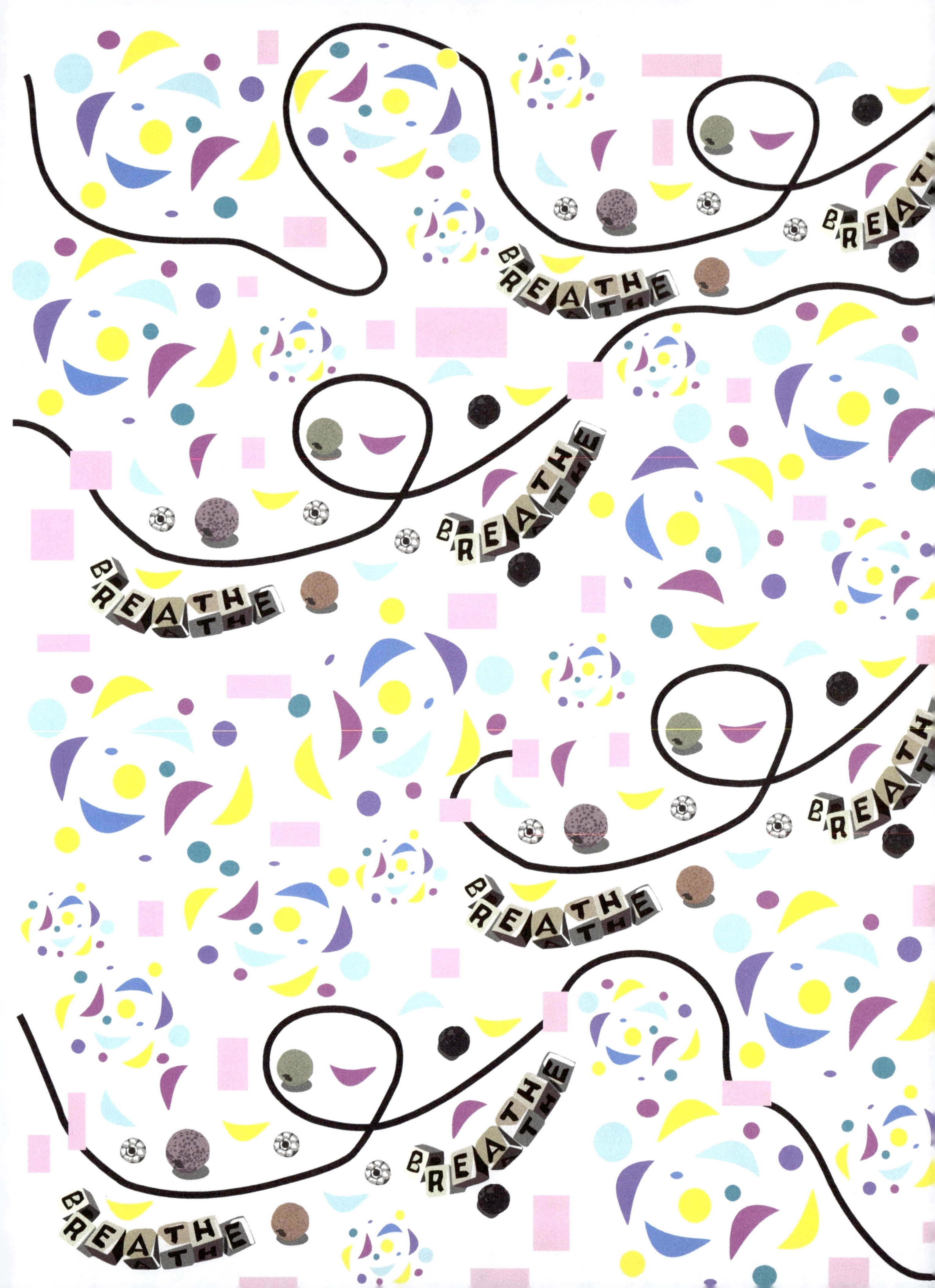
BREATH
BREATHE
BREATHE
BREATHE
BREATH
BREATHE
BREATHE
BREATHE

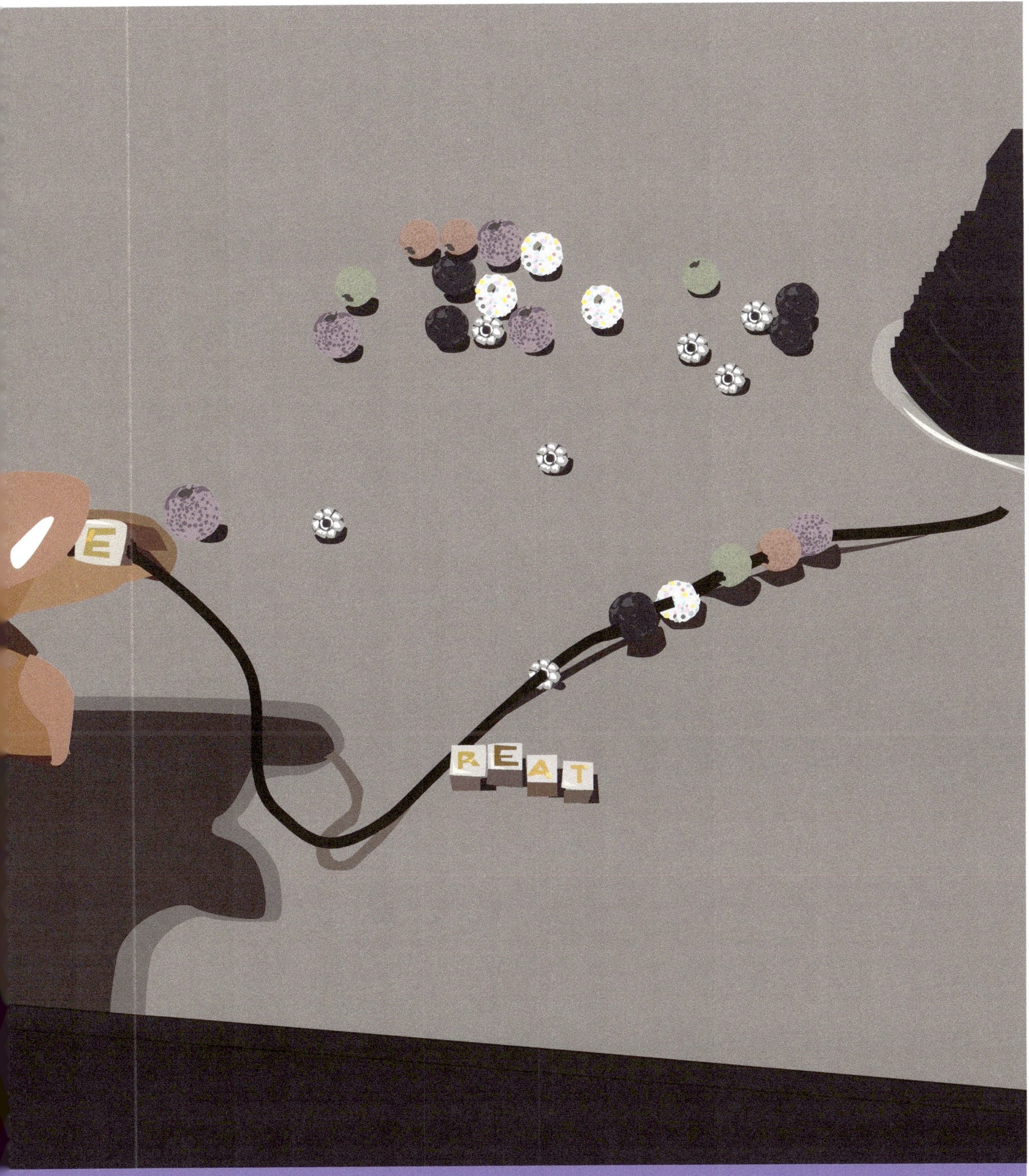


# Step Three

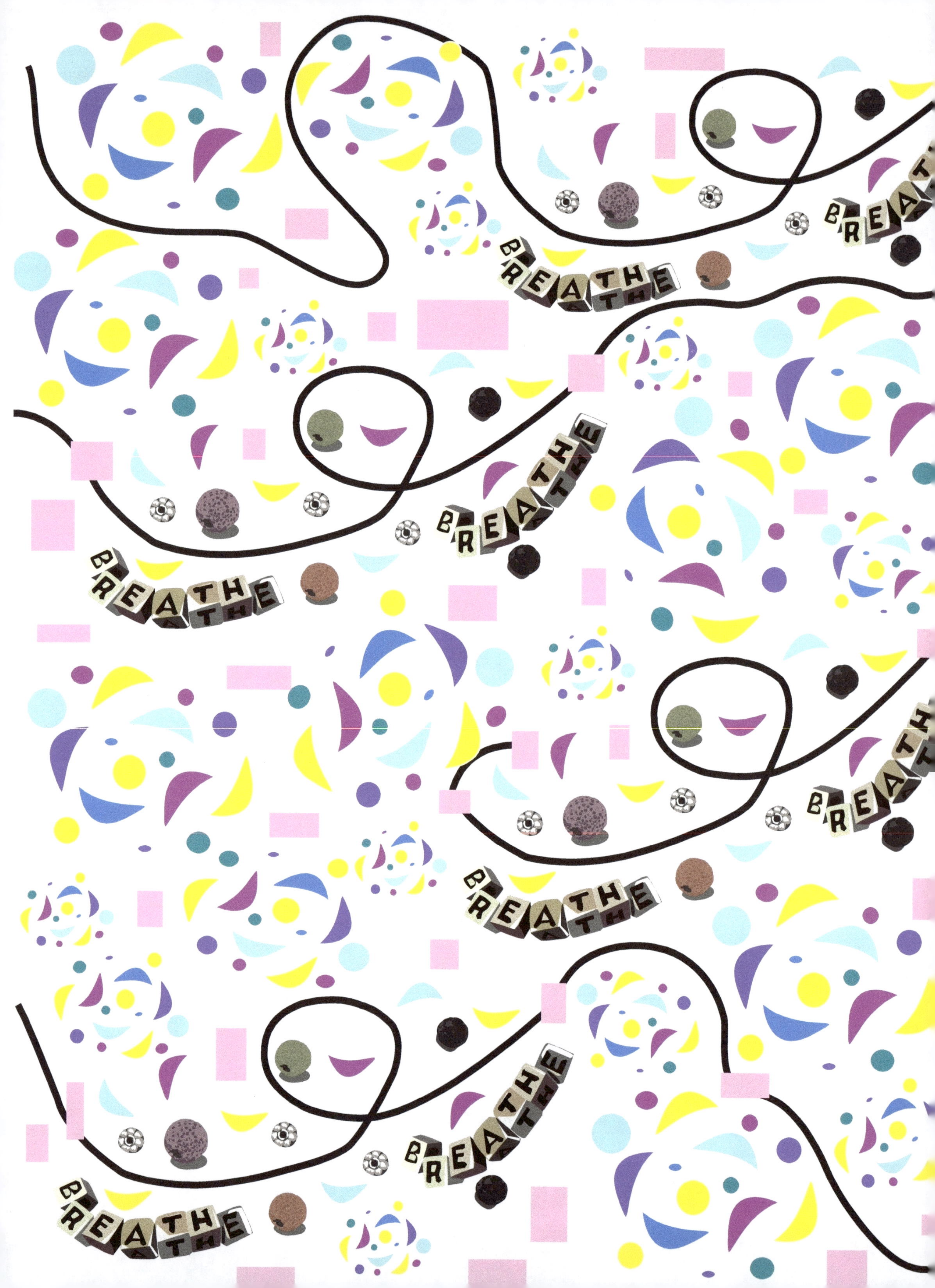
BREATHE
BREATHE
BREATHE
BREATHE
BREATHE
BREATHE
BREATHE
BREATHE

# Step Four

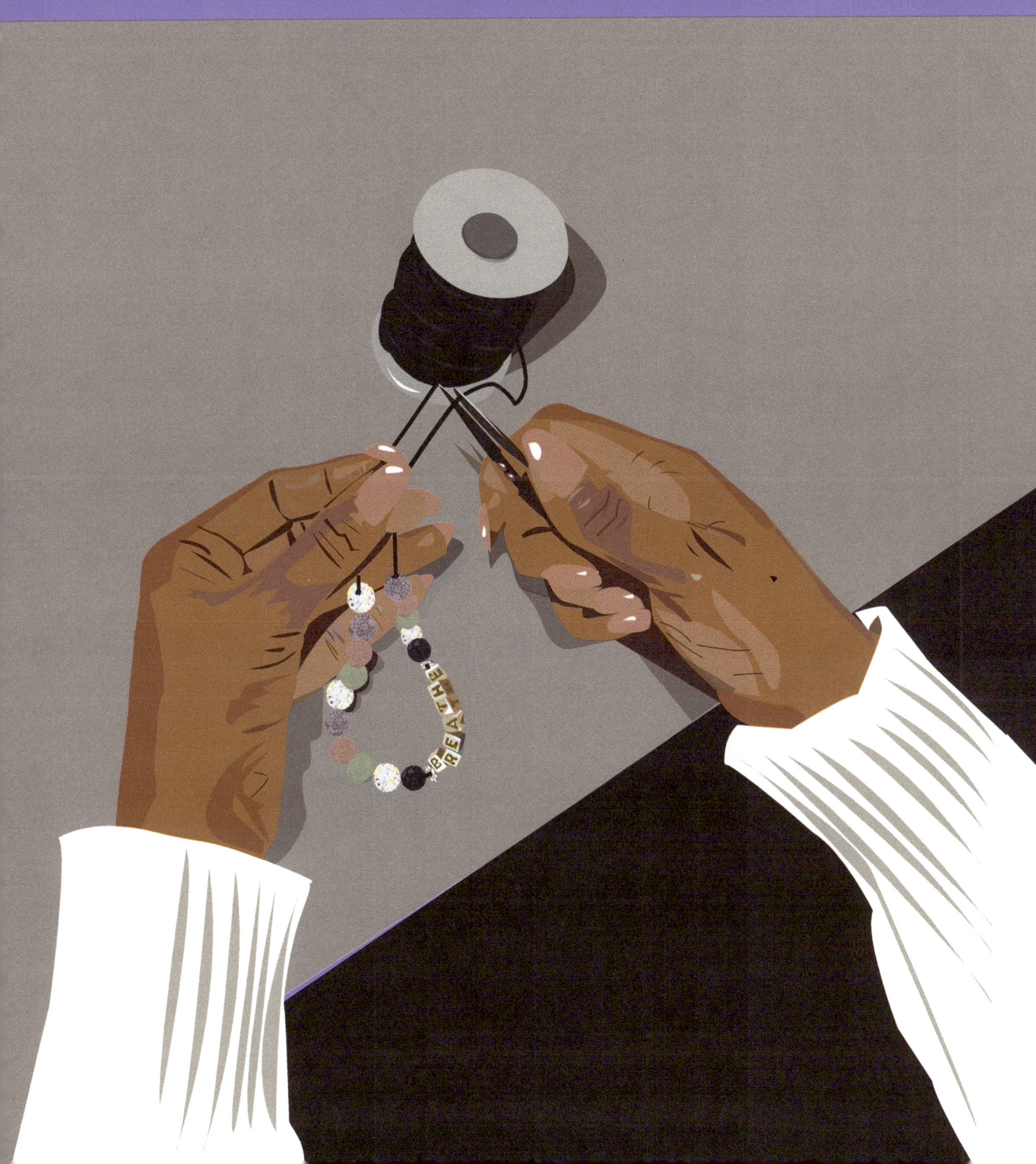

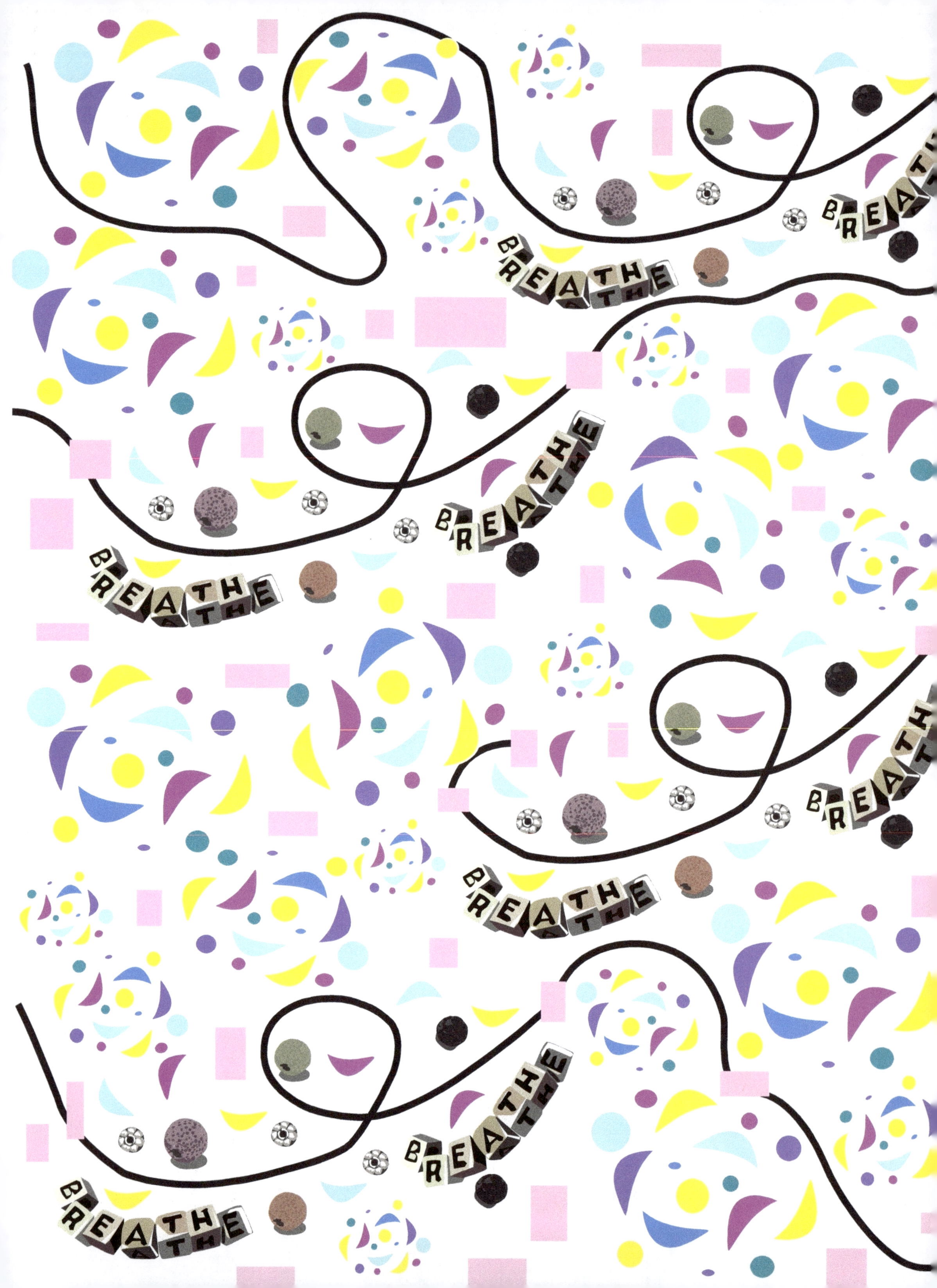
BREATHE
BREATHE
BREATHE
BREATHE
BREATHE
BREATHE

# Step Five

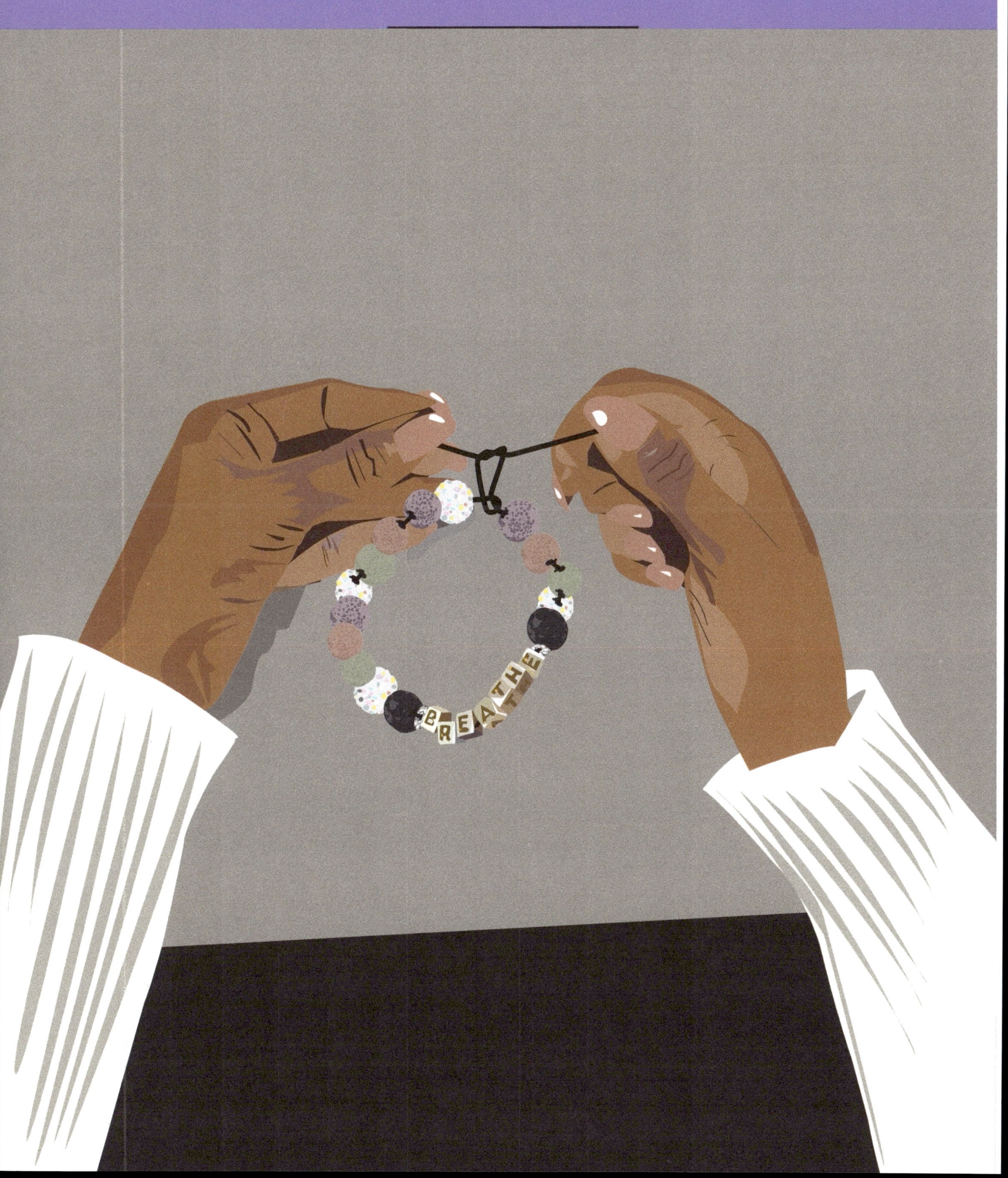

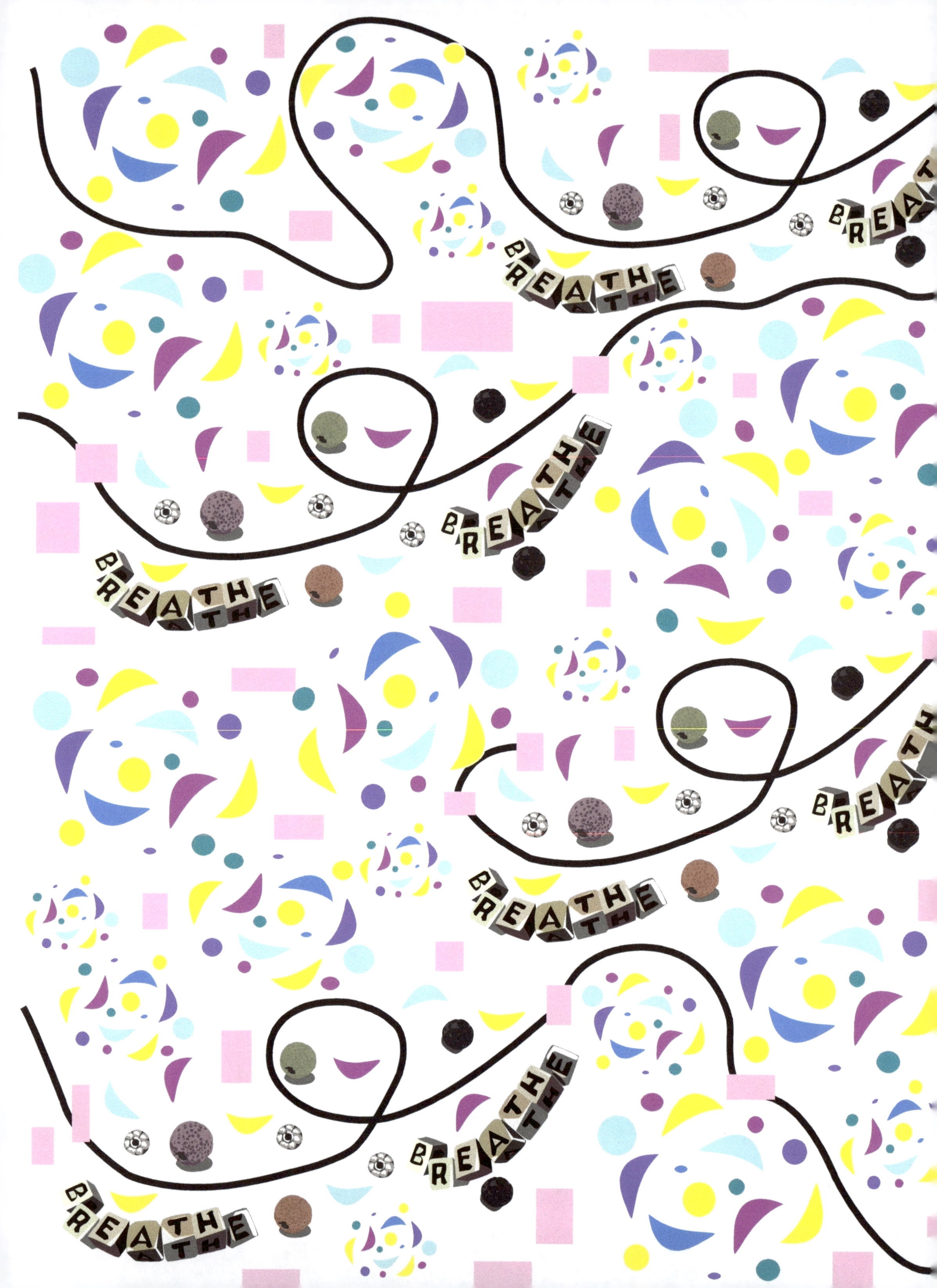
BREATHE
BREATHE
BREATHE
BREATHE
BREATHE
BREATHE

# Step Six

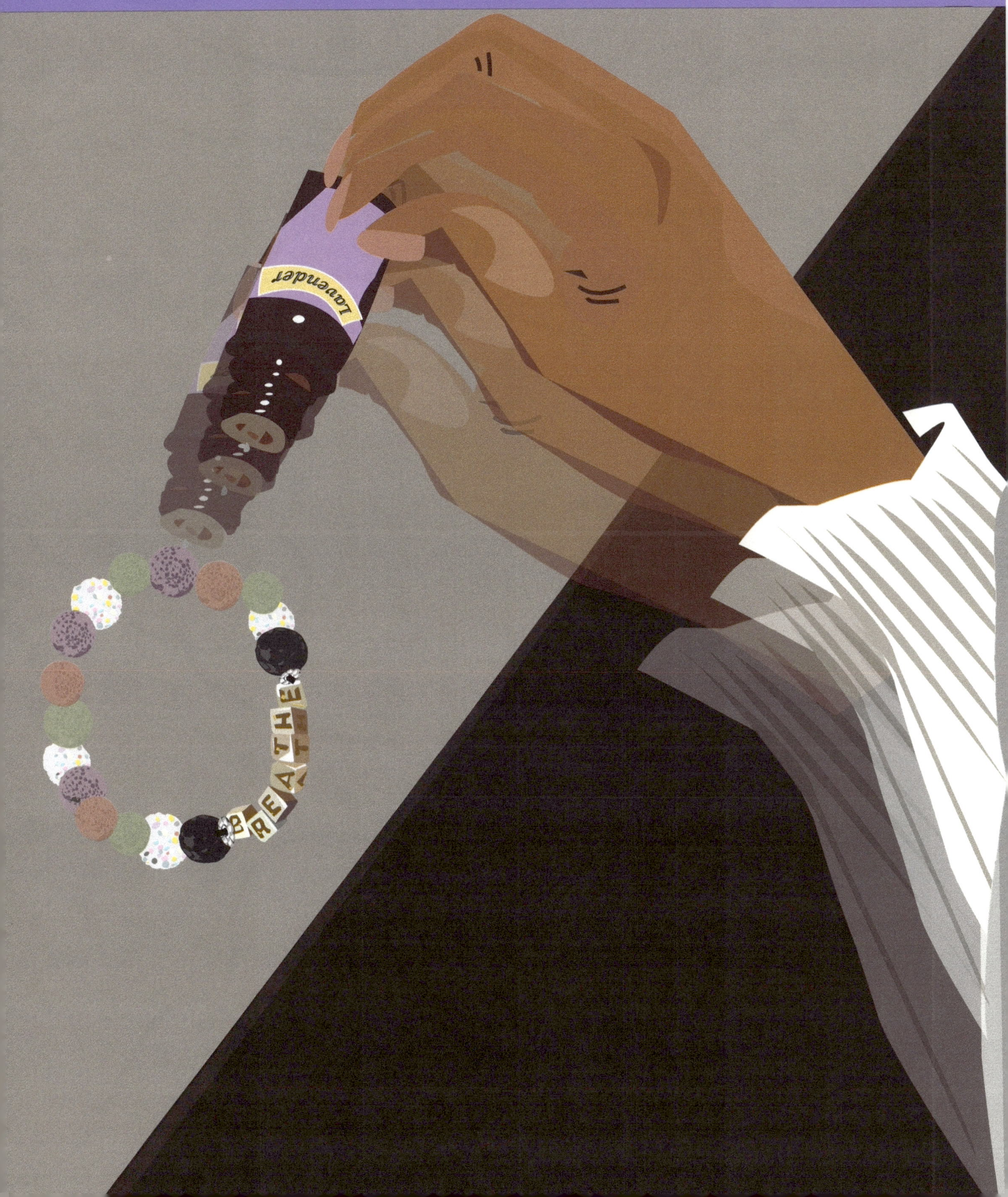

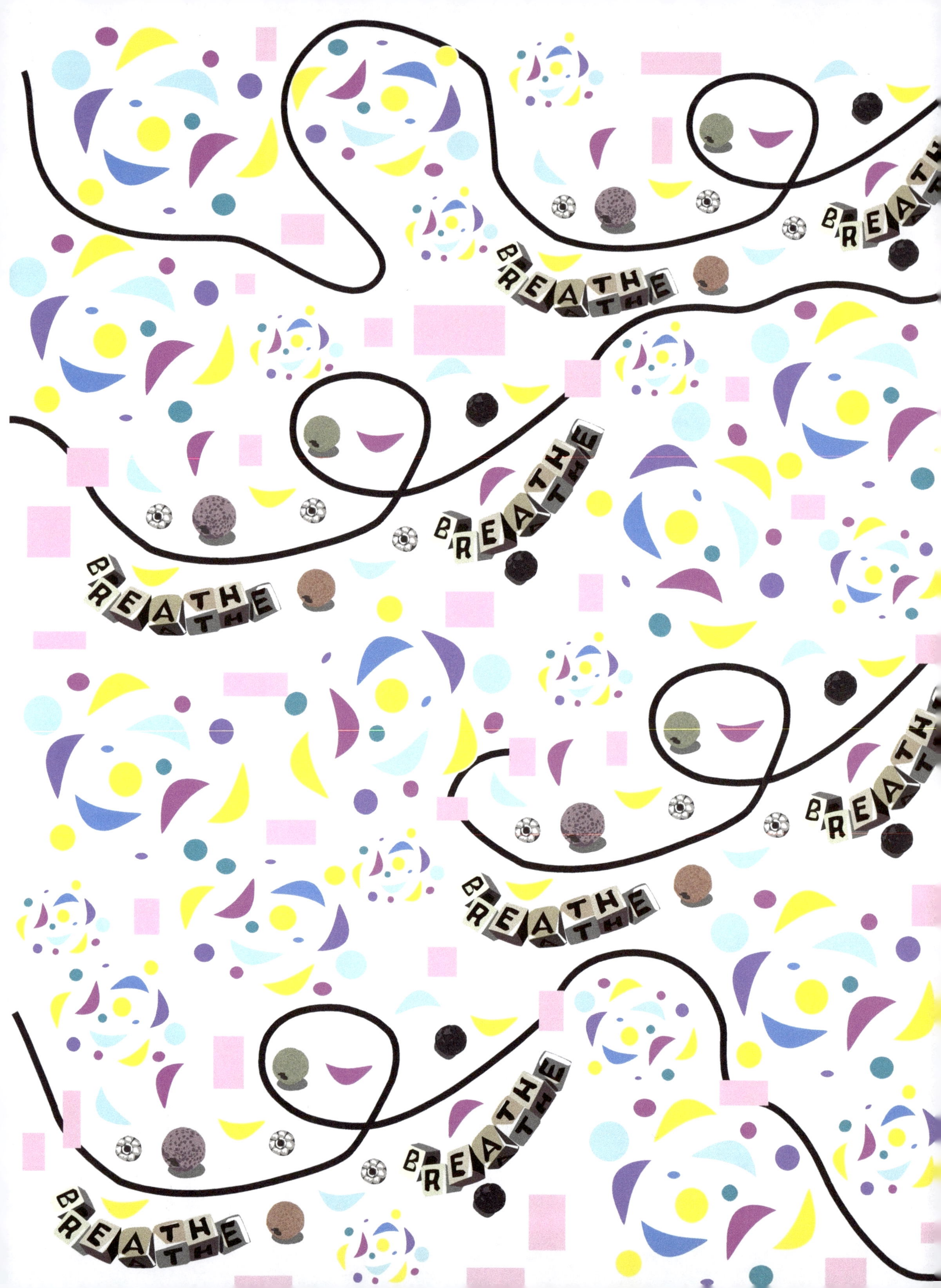
BREATHE
BREATHE
BREATHE
BREATHE
BREATHE
BREATHE

# Step Seven

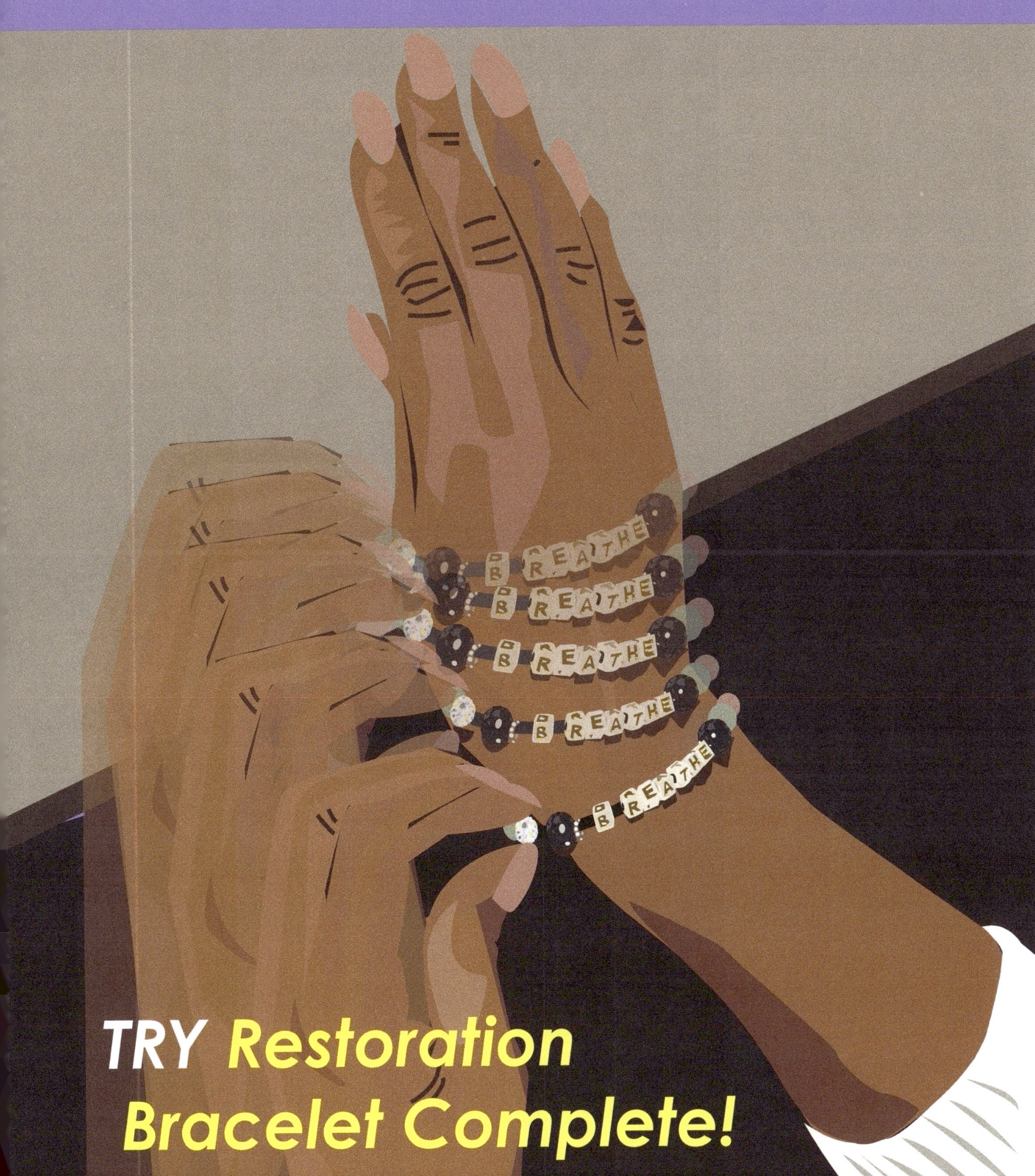

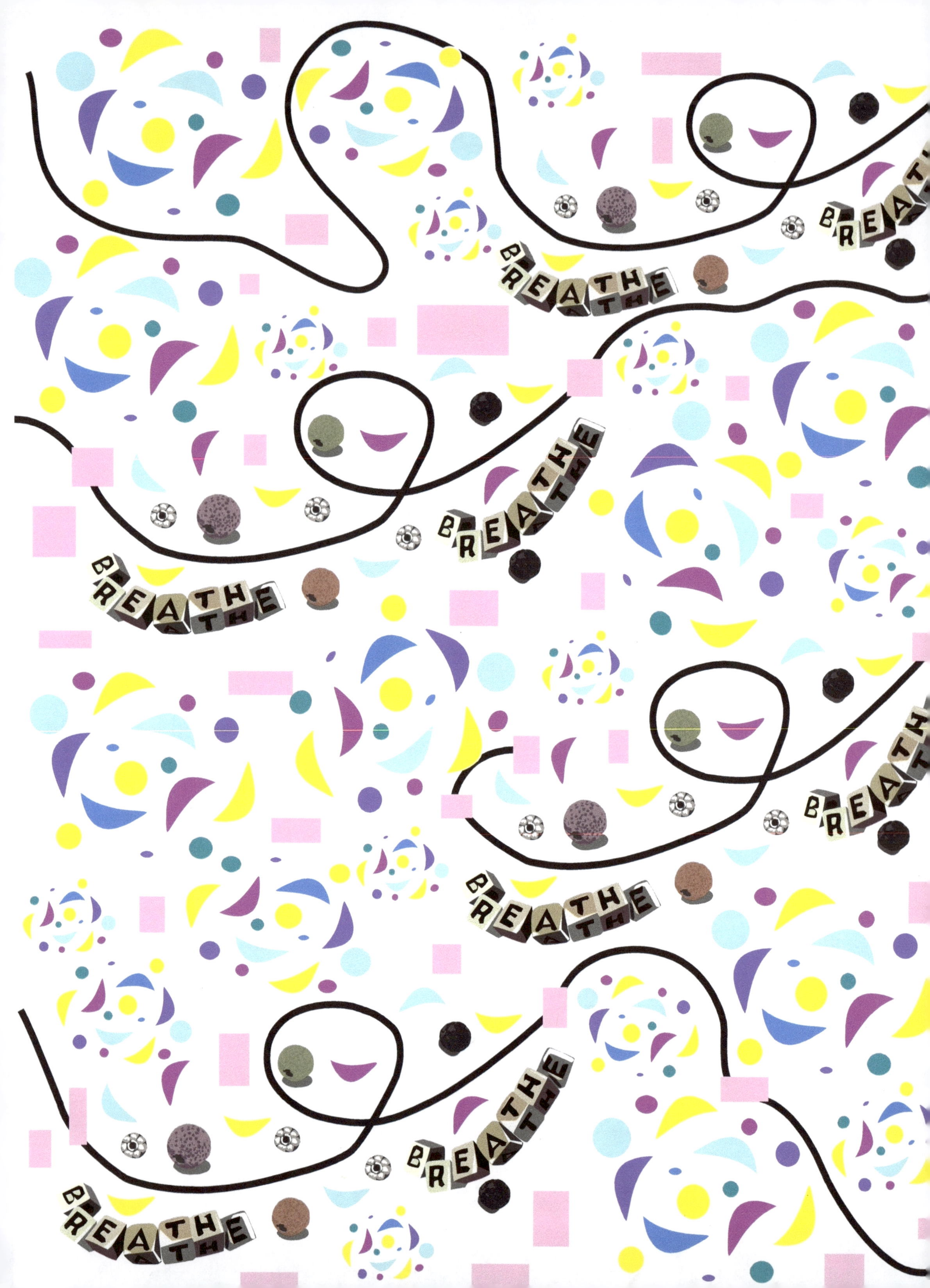
BREATHE

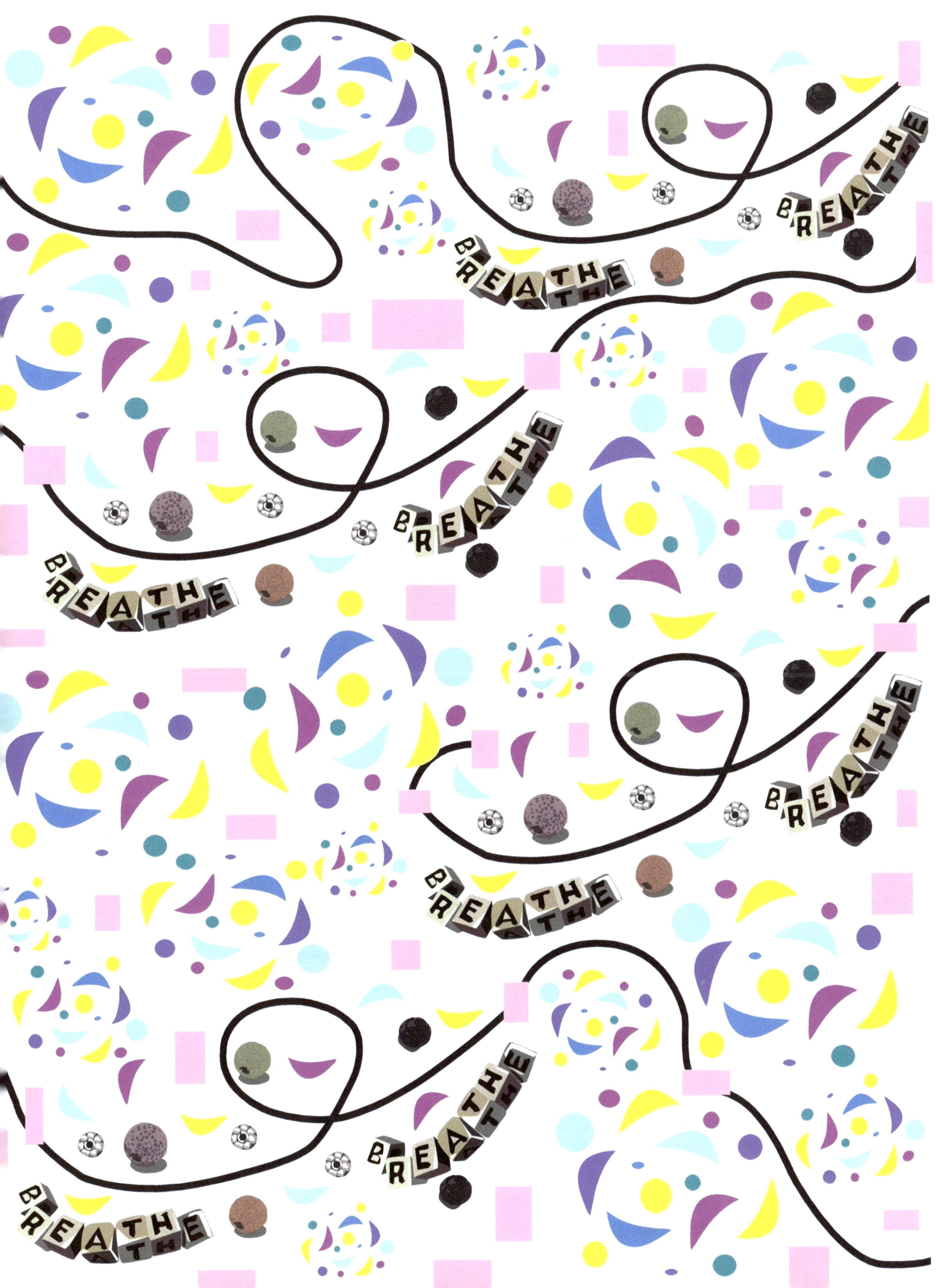
BREATHE
BREATHE
BREATHE
BREATHE
BREATHE
BREATHE
BREATHE
BREATHE

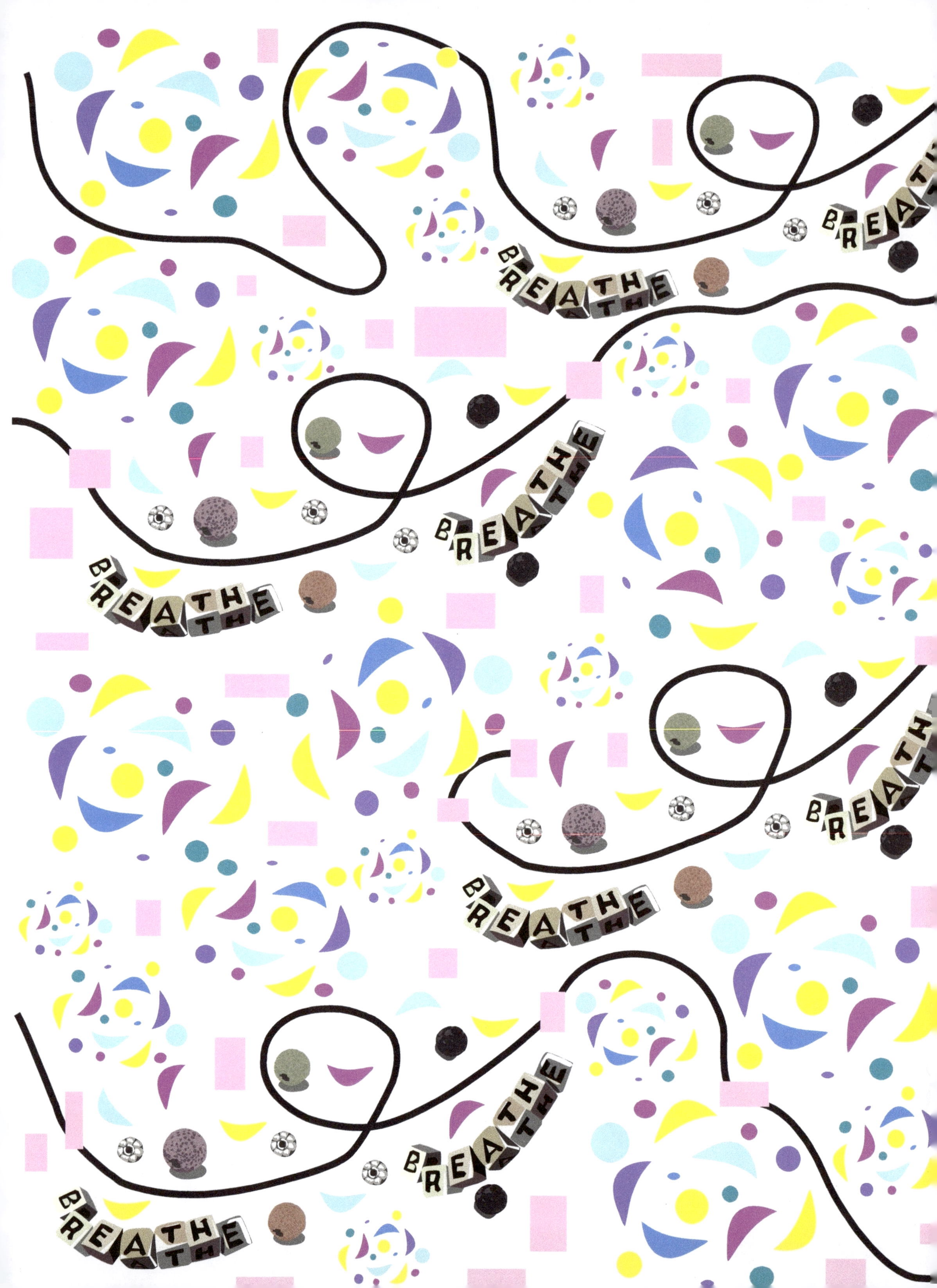
BREATHE
BREATHE
BREATHE
BREATHE
BREATHE
BREATHE
BREATHE
BREATHE

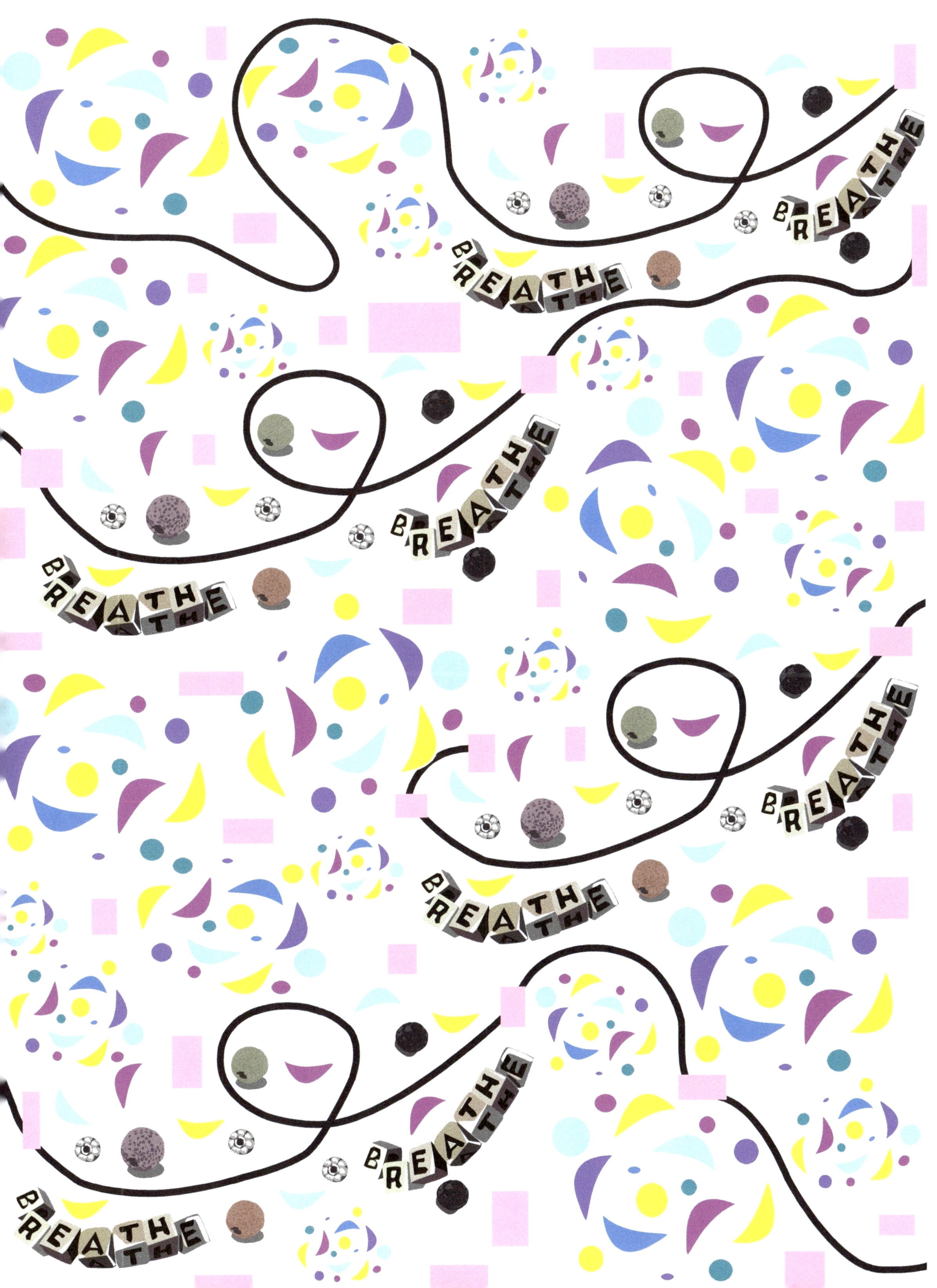
BREATHE
BREATHE
BREATHE
BREATHE
BREATHE
BREATHE
BREATHE
BREATHE

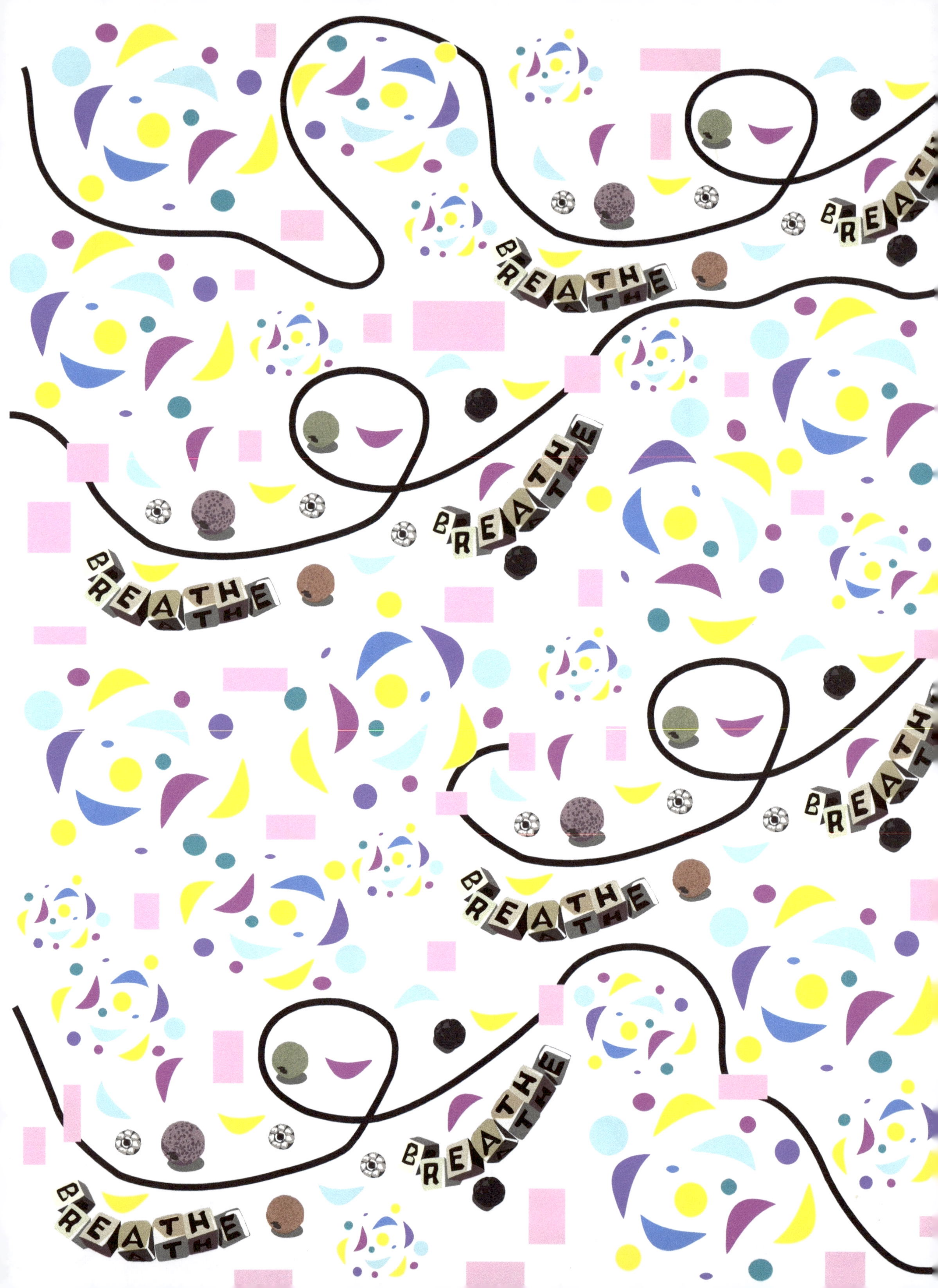
BREATHE
BREATHE
BREATHE
BREATHE
BREATHE
BREATHE

# Also Available

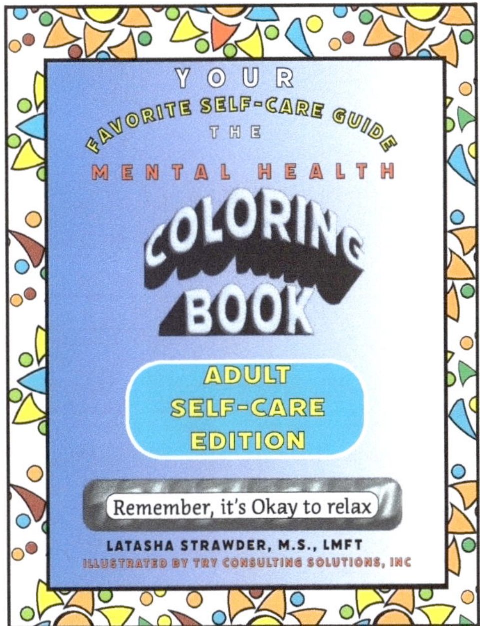


Order the
Self-Care Guide Here

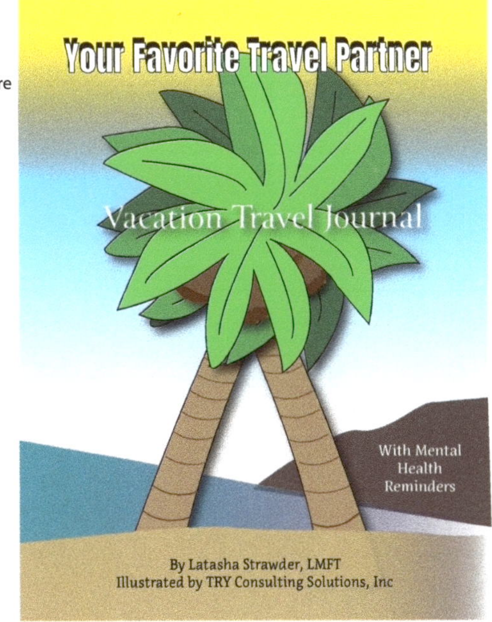


Order the
Mental Health
Travel Journal Here

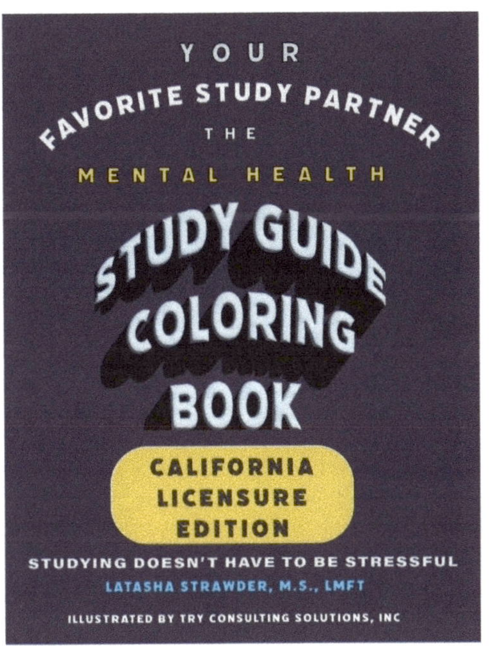


Order the
Study Guide
Coloring Book
Here

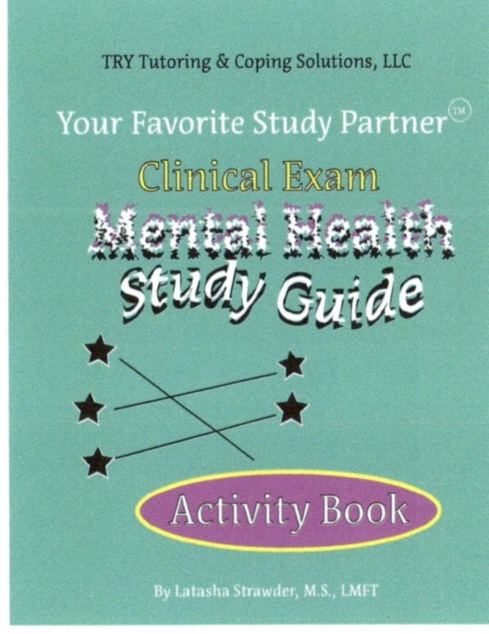


Order the
Mental Health
Activity Guide
Here

www.ingramcontent.com/pod-product-compliance
Lightning Source LLC
LaVergne TN
LVHW071451110826
845155LV00047B/20
* 9 7 9 8 9 8 8 5 2 2 6 3 8 *